EUROPA ✠ MILITARIA
SPECIAL Nº15

FRENCH FOREIGN LEGION
OPERATIONS 1990-2000

YVES DEBAY

The Crowood Press

This edition published in Great Britain 2000 by
The Crowood Press Ltd
Ramsbury, Marlborough, Wiltshire SN8 2HR

British Library Cataloguing-in-Publication Data
A catalogue record for this book is available
from the British Library

ISBN 1 86126 373 2

Edited by Martin Windrow
Designed by Torsten Verhülsdonk / VS Books
Printed and bound by Craft Print, Singapore.

Contents

Author's acknowledgements:
I should like to thank here all the officers, NCOs and men
of the French Foreign Legion for their support in researching
this book and their energetic assistance during the taking of
the photographs. Further thanks are due to the editorial staff
of *Képi Blanc* magazine for putting additional photographs
at my disposal, and to Carl Schulze for his photographs and
his comments on my text.

Dedication:
This book is dedicated to the more than 35,000 men of the
French Foreign Legion killed in action since the raising of
the corps in 1831.

Editor's note:
Consistent French capitalisation in an English text is
confusing to the reader. We have used English capitalisation
for the proper names and titles and the more familiar words
printed in Roman type - e.g. Légion, Régiment, képi,
légionnaire; and the uncapitalised French style for less
familiar terms printed in *italics*, e.g. *régiment de marche*, etc.

A Brief History of the Legion

'A Legion will be established consisting of foreigners. It will bear the title Foreign Legion.' So declared Article No 1 of the statute issued by King Louis Philippe of France on 10 March 1831, which marked the birth of the Foreign Legion.

Recruitment of foreign troops was traditional in France, and the first légionnaires came mostly from the recently disbanded Hohenlohe Regiment, which had incorporated former foreign units of Napoleon's army shortly after 1815. Six months later the Legion Étranger already comprised five national battalions, and was engaged in labouring and fighting in **Algeria**, invaded by France in 1830. Here, on 27 April 1832 at Maison Carré, legionnaires gained a victory which earned them their first flag.

The first tour in Algeria was followed in 1835-38 by service in the Carlist War in **Spain**, from which only 500 men out of 5,000 would return. During this campaign the battalions were mixed in nationality, and French became the official language of the Legion – both features which have been retained. In December 1835 it had been decided to recruit more foreigners for Algeria, and new battalions were shipped to North Africa in December 1836 and July 1837; third and fourth battalions were formed in December 1837 and October 1839, and 400 survivors of Spain volunteered to join this 'New Legion' on their return.

The conquest of **Algeria** lasted until June 1857, and during this period the Legion distinguished itself in battles such as Constantine (1837), Djidjelli (1839), Millianah (1840), Zaatcha (1849), and Ischeriden (1857). It also established a home for itself at Sidi-bel-Abbès near Oran. In 1854-56 the Legion also fought in the **Crimean War**, at the Alma and in the wretched siege of Sevastopol. Following service in **Italy** against the Austrians in 1859 the Legion took part for the first time in a triumphal march through Paris.

In 1863 the bulk of the Legion was shipped to Mexico to support France's puppet Emperor Maximilian. Over four years it distinguished itself in action many times, and when it was shipped back to Algeria it left behind 2,002 dead officers and men. It was here that the Legion, previously a disregarded corps which was often neglected and used for the most unhealthy or dangerous missions, established its legend – not least in the small but desperate battle of Camerone (see page 7) – and its distinctive identity within the French army.

In 1870-71 légionnaires defended French soil for the first time in the **Franco Prussian War**. After helping to quash unrest on its return to Algeria, from 1883 onwards the Legion provided regular battalions, or specially formed *régiments de marche* ('task forces' assembled from men of the garrison units), for many of France's campaigns of imperial expansion. These expeditions included **Tonkin** (1883), **Formosa** (1885), **Soudan** in north-west Africa – today's Mali and Niger (1892-93), **Dahomey** (1892-94), **Siam** (1893-97), **Madagascar** (1895-1905); and, in particular, **Morocco** (1900-1934).

The insignia and decorations worn on summer parade uniform by this long-serving *adjudant* or company sergeant-major of the 3e REI (3rd Foreign Infantry Regiment) tell a story about his regiment's history as well as his own career. The black and red képi with silver and gold lace ornaments is worn by senior NCOs and officers, as are the black shoulder-boards with lace rank stripes. Above his right pocket are the large gold *brevet de montagne* marking his personal qualification as an army mountain guide, above the US Presidential Citation awarded to the 3e REI's World War II predecessor, the RMLE, which saw hard fighting in Alsace in winter 1944-45.

Fobbed to the pocket is the regimental badge. High on his left breast is the gold *brevet de chef de section* of a qualified platoon leader. The triple *fourragère* or lanyard – in the ribbon colours of the Légion d'Honneur, Médaille Militaire and Croix de Guerre 1914-18 – marks the 16 citations in Army Orders gained by the regiment since such distinctions were introduced during World War I. His personal medals include the Croix de Guerre TOE ('for external theatres of operations') and its later replacement, the Croix de Valeur Militaire; the Médaille d'Outre-Mer, the Médaille de Defense Nationale, and the Saudi Arabian medal for the liberation of Kuwait in 1991.

After fighting to capture these new possessions the Legion units often remained to garrison them, and played a major part in both policing and developing the newly occupied territories. During this period the Legion's tradition was solidly established: légionnaires could make themselves at home anywhere on earth, and still pride themselves today on their

Every légionnaire spends at least two years of his contract overseas. Here men of the 13e DBLE dismount from their VLRA light recce and support truck in the inhospitable desert of Djibouti in the 'Horn of Africa'. Amongst the visible weapons are the FAMAS assault rifle, FR F-2 sniper rifle, F-1 machine gun and LRAC 89mm anti-armour rocket launcher.

skills not only in combat but as builders and craftsmen who have left their barracks and monuments all over the world.

The outbreak of **World War I** found the Legion with 12 battalions, and more were quickly formed with 'duration only' volunteers. Most légionnaires fought in France, but a battalion was engaged in the Dardanelles and later in Bulgaria and Serbia. The units committed on the Western Front were brought together on 11 November 1915 into a single three-battalion Régiment de Marche de la Légion Étrangère (RMLE). Under the leadership, from April 1917, of Lt Col Paul Rollet, the RMLE greatly distinguished itself in many battles, and its nine citations in Army Orders made it (equal with the Moroccan Colonial Infantry Regiment) the most decorated regiment in the French army.

Rollet, who spent his entire career from lieutenant to general in the Legion, was its first Inspector – a post created especially for him in 1931. Known as the 'Father of the Legion', he worked tirelessly for the improvement, the welfare and the reputation of his corps.

During 1914-18 the under-strength Legion units left in **Morocco** saw hard marching and hard fighting to hold down the restless tribes. When the Legion returned from the Western Front new regiments were organised, and battalions campaigned in Morocco until its final pacification in 1934. In 1920-21 a cavalry regiment was raised for the first time; and men of this 1er REC also distinguished themselves in Syria.

In **World War II** the Franco-German armistice of 1940 left far-flung Legion garrisons under Vichy control, and the changing fortunes of war brought them both disasters and triumphs. To summarise briefly: Legion units fought the Germans in Norway and France (1940); war-raised units in France were disbanded immediately after the armistice; the 13e Demi-Brigade de Legion Étrangère (13e DBLE) sided with De Gaulle, and fought alongside the British in Eritrea and Syria (1941), in the Western Desert (especially at Bir Hakeim and El Alamein, 1942), and in Italy (1943). The Anglo-US invasion of French North Africa and the subsequent fighting in Tunisia (1943) brought the Legion garrison into the Allied camp; re-organised and re-equipped along American lines, the second RMLE fought from the south of France up through Alsace-Lorraine, and ended the war in Austria.

VE-Day brought the Legion only a brief respite before deployment of much of its strength to **Indochina**, where the communist Viet Minh movement resisted the return of French rule. Between 1946 and 1954 the war escalated from guerrilla pinpricks to major operations in divisional strength, with naval and air support. 1948 saw the raising of the Legion's élite 1st Parachute Battalion, soon followed by a second (1er & 2e BEP). Legion infantry, armoured cavalry and parachute units fought in all the main campaigns throughout Indochina, at a cost of 314 officers and 10,168 NCOs and men – and it was légionnaires of the 3e REI who provided the final resistance in strongpoint 'Isabelle' at Dien Bien Phu on 8 May 1954.

On their return to their bases in **Algeria** the Legion found their next war already beginning – the savage struggle for Algerian independence from France was to last until 1962, and the Legion was heavily engaged throughout, at a cost of 65 officers and 1,911 NCOs and men. Algerian independence

---

ACTIVE UNITS OF THE FOREIGN LEGION

Administrative and training:
Commandement de la Legion Étrangère (COM.LE)
1er Régiment Étranger (1er RE)
4e Régiment Étranger (4e RE)

Rapid Action Force (FAR), subordinate to
6th Light Armoured Division (6e DLB):
1er Régiment Étranger de Cavalerie (1er REC)
2e Régiment Étranger d'Infanterie (2e REI)
6e Régiment Étranger du Génie (6e REG)

Rapid Action Force, subordinate to
11th Parachute Division (11e DP):
2e Régiment Étranger de Parachutistes (2e REP)

Stationed overseas:

At Kourou, French Guiana, subordinate to
Forces Armées aux Antilles-Guyane:
3e Régiment Étranger d'Infanterie (3e REI)

On Hao Atoll, Polynesia, subordinate to COMSUP:
5e Régiment Étranger (5e RE)

In Djibouti, subordinate to Forces Francaises de Djibouti:
13e Démi-Brigade de Légion Étrangère (13e DBLE)

On Mayotte, Comores Islands, subordinate to
Forces Armées dans la Zone Sud de l'Ocean Indien:
Détachement de Légion Étrangère de Mayotte (DLEM)

Today's légionnaires are specialists, who dominate the battlefield as much by sophisticated electronics as by firepower. This 2e REP paratrooper feeds reconnaissance data into a laptop; it will subsequently be transmitted to tactical HQ over a portable satellite radio link. Recce targets are also photographed, to give operation planners the most detailed possible view of the terrain.

also cost the Legion its home at Sidi-bel-Abbès. Garrisons were established in France and Corsica, South America, East Africa, and on islands in the Indian Ocean and the Pacific, with the central depot and 1er RE at Aubagne near Marseilles in southern France.

Up to the beginning of the 1990s Legion units saw active service in **Chad** in 1969-70 and 1978-88, on the **Djibouti/Somalia** border, in the famous hostage rescue operation by the 2e REP at Kolwezi in the **Congo** in 1978, and in UN operations in **Lebanon** in 1983. In the first few generations of its 160-year existence the Legion had developed from a disregarded labour corps into a fighting élite, committed in all theatres of war where there was a French presence. The modern Legion had now found a new role for itself in the aftermath of imperial disengagement, evolving from garrison troops into spearhead units of paratroops, light and mechanised infantry, armoured cavalry and engineers, for rapid intervention overseas wherever French foreign policy required.

The Legion Today

The Legion's attention to its history and traditions – particularly promoted by General Rollet in the 1920s-30s, and ever since – helps weld together men of well over 100 nationalities into a military family, forming a distinct part of the French army: *Legio Patria Nostra*, 'The legion is our homeland'. The minor traditions of everyday life are as cherished as the major festivals - the slow marching pace inherited from the Hohenlohe Regiment; the Christmas festivities in which all ranks take part together; the white képi, blue sash and fringed green/red epaulettes of the légionnaire's parade uniform, and insignia recalling the lineage of the individual regiments; and the great annual parade on Camerone Day.

In 1997, 8,200 men served in the Foreign Legion, of which 350 were officers. The soldiers were of 138 nationalities, of which only 42% spoke French as their mother tongue. Every year an average of 8,500 men apply to enlist in the Legion, of whom only perhaps one in six – about 1,200 – survive the selection process and are accepted for basic training. The average applicant is 23 years old, and his nationality will reflect the world's current political and economic situation.

Legion special forces units employ all methods of infiltration, including diving. Here a scuba-equipped DINOPS team from the 6e REG check the compass before the underwater phase of a mission.

Thus, immediately after World War II the Legion had a high proportion of Germans; and today 30% of applicants come from Eastern Europe. Their reasons are as diverse as their backgrounds. They may simply seek better living conditions, or escape from a domestic or financial crisis; the Legion offers them adventure, comradeship, and a new sense of self-worth.

It should be emphasised that the modern, highly selective Legion does not offer a refuge for those who have committed serious crimes. Minor offences in an applicant's past are

CODE OF HONOUR OF THE LÉGIONNAIRE

Légionnaire, you serve France as a volunteer, with honour and loyalty.

Every légionnaire is your brother in arms, irrespective of his nationality, race, or religion. As a member of the same family you must always show him unshakable solidarity.

Be respectful of your traditions and conscious of your duty to your superiors. Discipline and comradeship are your strength, courage and loyalty your virtue.

Be proud of being a légionnaire, and express this through your uniform: always be smartly turned-out. Your conduct should always be dignified but modest, and your quarters always clean.

As an élite soldier, train with real severity; treat your weapons with the greatest respect, and maintain your physical condition tirelessly.

The mission is sacred: carry it through to the end, at any cost.

In battle, comport yourself without passion and without hatred. Show respect for the defeated enemy. Never abandon the dead, the wounded, or weapons.

tolerated; but the record of every would-be légionnaire is thoroughly checked through Interpol before he is accepted.

Who can apply? The candidate must be between 17 and 40 years old, with valid identity papers, and if still a minor must provide permission from his parents or educational authorities. There are no limits of nationality, creed or colour (except that Frenchmen are not formally accepted – they must present themselves as Belgians, Swiss, etc.). Physical fitness is essential, but knowledge of the French language is not – language instruction forms part of basic training. The selection process takes place at the 1er RE depot at Aubagne.

If the candidate passes the medical, physical and aptitude tests and the checking of criminal records, he signs an initial contract for five years' service including two years overseas.

From the 1er RE he is transferred to the 4e RE for his four months' basic training, after which he is posted to an operational regiment according to his capabilities and the needs of the Legion. On arrival he receives the necessary specialist training, e.g. parachuting, sniping marksmanship, etc. For any necessary technical training – e.g. vehicle maintenance, tele-communications skills, etc. – he will be posted back to the 4e RE, which carries out this training centrally for the whole corps.

During the signing-on process any légionnaire who expresses the wish to be *'anonymat'* receives a new name, and can also be listed under a new nationality and date of birth; this option is often exercised by Frenchmen – theoretically disqualified from enlistment – but also by any other applicant who wishes to make a clean break with his former life. After three years the légionnaire may reverse this decision at his own choice, or may keep his new identity until retirement.

On leaving the Legion the former légionnaire has the option of choosing French citizenship. After 15 years' service he qualifies for a small pension, which is increased for 20 years' service. This term also brings entitlement for entry to the Institution des Invalides, a Legion old soldiers' home at Puyloubier near Aubagne; this is self-supporting by the produce of its farms, e.g. the wine which is retailed in Legion canteens. However, retirement need not end any man's contact with the Legion; in most countries he may join a veterans' association, and news about the Legion's world-wide family is available through the monthly magazine *Képi Blanc*.

The Future

The units of the Legion are integrated into the formations of the French regular army, using the same equipment and operating under a common chain of command. After the recent announcement of the abolition of compulsory conscription to the French forces the structure of the new all-professional army will change. The restructuring provides for a reduction of units, and the former divisional organisation will be broken down into brigades. For the Legion, however, the re-organisation actually means enlargement; a new engineer regiment is being formed. The 2e REI is to be increased to eight companies, and apart from its intervention role will also trial all new French infantry equipment.

Regimental police of the 2e REI during the regiment's 150th anniversary celebrations. The old Willys jeep and its French-built version have given the Legion good service all over the world for more than 50 years, and a few are still to be seen alongside the modern P4 all-terrain vehicle.

Camerone

In 1863 France sent a large expeditionary force to Mexico to support the puppet Emperor Maximilian whom she had placed on the throne, but who was stubbornly resisted by those Mexicans who remained loyal to President Juarez. Among these troops were the bulk of the Foreign Legion, led by Colonel Jeanningros. While most of the army was laying siege to the city of Puebla, the légionnaires were strung out to protect the lines of supply through the disease-ridden lowlands between Puebla and the port of Vera Cruz, with headquarters at Chiquihuite.

A month after their arrival Jeanningros was informed that an important convoy carrying gold and siege equipment was coming up from the coast on 30 April; and he ordered the 3rd Company of the 1st Battalion to march back from Chiquihuite to ensure the security of the route and to meet and escort the convoy. Fever had already reduced the company to 62 NCOs and men, and all its officers were sick; so command was taken by three officers from the headquarters - Captain Jean Danjou, and Sous-lieutenants Vilain and Maudet. All were veterans: Danjou had worn a wooden left hand since the accidental explosion of a gun in the Crimea, and both the subalterns were promoted ex-rankers.

The company marched at 1am on 30 April 1863. Halting at 6am to rest and make coffee in scrubland near Palo Verde, they saw approaching 800 Juarista cavalry under Colonel de Paula Milan, intent on ambushing the convoy. Danjou fell back on the cover offered by the nearby ruined hamlet of Camaron (Camerone), forming a moving square and beating off the first cavalry attacks. Before the company reached the ruins the mules carrying their rations, spare water and ammunition had bolted. Since the légionnaires had already emptied their canteens into the cooking pots to make coffee, they faced dreadful thirst under the blazing Mexican sun.

The ruins consisted of an abandoned two-storey hacienda and a 45m (150ft) square enclosure, its walls – breeched at three points – partly lined with ramshackle lean-to stables. Juarist snipers were already in place in upper rooms of the hacienda. Danjou's men turned Camerone into a makeshift fort, and he refused an offer of surrender. The dismounted cavalry, armed with carbines, attacked at about 9.30am but were driven off. At mid-morning Captain Danjou was shot in

On 1 May 1863 Colonel Jeanningros and a relief column found the terribly wounded Drummer Lai hiding in the scrub; the jumbled, stripped corpses of the defenders of Camerone; and, amid the grim debris of battle, Captain Jean Danjou's wooden hand. Ever since it has remained the Legion's most honoured relic,

the symbol of sacrifice, of the keeping of one's given word, and of the sacredness of the mission whatever the price. It is kept in the Salle d'Honneur, and is paraded – carried by a highly decorated veteran and a carefully selected young légionnaire – during the solemn ceremony at the Legion's main depot each 30 April.

the chest; before dying he made his men promise to fight to the last. Surrounded and under fire from all sides, the company stood off further attacks; and at about midday the Juarists brought up three battalions totalling some 1,200 infantry. Vilain refused another surrender demand, and led the defence until he too was killed in mid-afternoon, shot by Mexican snipers from the upper storey of the main building. Each enemy rush left more of the little perimeter under close fire, and more French dead; the wounded strewn around the yard, tortured by thirst, licked their own blood; and the cartridge pouches steadily emptied.

By about 5pm Maudet had just 11 men left, penned in the lean-to stables, down to their last rounds, and choking in the smoke from the now-burning hacienda. Cursing his men for cowards, a Mexican commander prepared for the final attack. Ten kilometres to the east Captain Cabossel, leading the convoy, was warned by his Indian scouts of the battle at Camerone. With only two companies himself, he had no choice but to retrace his path to Le Soledad in safety.

At about 6pm Sous-lieutenant Maudet and four men still resisted: Corporal Maine and Légionnaires Catteau, Constantin and Wenzel. As the Mexicans swarmed towards them they fired their last rounds – and charged with fixed bayonets ...Maudet fell, wounded twice, and Catteau died immediately; Maine, Constantin and Wenzel stood over them. Restraining his men, the Juarist Colonel Combas offered them a last chance to surrender; Maine replied that they would accept only if they could keep their weapons, and if their wounded could be cared for. Combas is supposed to have replied, 'I can refuse nothing to men like you'; and when he took these last three men before Colonel de Paula Milan the latter exclaimed that these were devils, not men. Maine and 11 other légionnaires survived captivity, and one other man was found alive – with nine wounds – by the relief column which arrived next day.

In a battle lasting 12 hours the 65 légionnaires had resisted more than 2,000 enemy, and had fulfilled their mission to safeguard the convoy. For the Legion, Camerone remains the ultimate example of duty, loyalty, and the fulfilment of the mission at any cost. 30 April is celebrated by all Legion units wherever they find themselves, in peace or war; the greatest ceremonial takes place at the 1er RE depot at Aubagne, where a solemn parade and a generously lubricated feast are attended by thousands of former officers and légionnaires from all over the world.

1er Régiment Étranger

As the Legion's oldest unit, dating from 10 March 1831, the 1st Foreign Regiment is the guardian of the Legion's traditions. Throughout the period 1831-1918 it fought in all the campaigns in Algeria, where it built and occupied the Legion's headquarters at Sidi-bel-Abbès. The 1er RE also provided troops to fight in Spain, the Crimea, Italy, Mexico, the Franco-Prussian War, Tonkin, Dahomey, French West Africa (Soudan), Madagascar, Morocco, and the trenches of the Western Front. When the Legion returned from World War I, the 1er REI (1st Foreign Infantry Regiment – reverted to 1st Foreign Regiment, 1er RE, in 1955) took over central administrative and training tasks for the whole Legion, while still providing combat battalions as needed.

After World War II the regiment – at first at Sidi-bel-Abbès and from 1962 at Aubagne – formed the basis for the reception and training of tens of thousands of légionnaires, and their subsequent transfer to the units fighting in Indochina and Algeria. Although training is carried out today by the 4e RE, the légionnaire's service still begins and ends at the 1er RE's Quartier Viénot, the 'mother-house' of the Legion (most Legion barracks are named after officers killed in battle; Colonel Viénot fell in the Crimea).

The 1er RE is divided into four companies. The Regimental Command & Services Company has about 350 officers and men divided into 20 cells, together providing the unit's administrative framework. The company also trains men in specialist administrative skills before their transfer to other units. The CCSR is also responsible for the Pioneers, who lead Legion parades.

The Foreign Legion Services Company (CSLE) has some 370 of all ranks; known as 'the general's company', it regulates the Legion's headquarters command staff, and deals with personnel matters. This company is also responsible for the 14-day candidate selection process, managing the Centre for Selection & Incorporation (CSI). The CSLE is also

(Top of page) Regimental breast and beret badges of the 1er RE; the former has the eagle and serpent motif of Mexico, recalling the campaign of 1863-67.

(Below) The pioneer platoon of the 1er RE traditionally opens the Camerone Day parade at Aubagne. The festival is honoured by every unit or detachment, but the most spectacular celebration is naturally at the *'maison mére'*, Quartier Viénot.

(Above) The grand ceremonial which marks each 30 April was born – like the formal celebration of many Legion traditions – in the Legion's centenary year of 1931, when General Rollet went to great lengths to establish his corps' unique identity in the public mind; but Camerone Day celebrations had been recorded at unit level since 1906. Here the Musique Principale plays on Camerone 1990 by the Monument aux Morts on the parade ground at the Quartier Viénot.

The Legion's Monument to the Dead was another of General Rollet's projects. On a massive dark bronze globe of the world, flanked by four huge figures, the countries where the Legion has fought are gilded. Every 30 April the veteran who has the honour of carrying the wooden hand of Captain Danjou reads aloud the story of the battle, the official Récit de Camerone.

(Right) The Musique Principale parade on Camerone Day. The trumpet and drum banners are in the Legion's traditional colours of red and green, and bear the corps' badge of a seven-flamed grenade and the Latin motto LEGIO PATRIA NOSTRA – 'The legion is our homeland'. While it appears on the regimental badge of the 3e REI, this is the motto of the Legion as a whole.

The principal march – we might even say the hymn – of the Legion is *Le Boudin*. Its origins are unknown, but it predates the Mexican campaign of 1863. The name means 'the blood sausage' or 'black pudding', and the words of the first verse are cheerful but obscure: *'Well, there's the sausage, there's the sausage, there's the sausage/ For the Alsatians, the Swiss and the Lorrainers/ There's none left for the Belgians/ There's none left for the Belgians/ Because they're shirkers....'* This lyric does not seem to match one theory put forward to explain the name – that it refers to the tentroll strapped to the old légionnaires' huge packs.

9

(Above) The Musique Principale has some traditions not found in other French military bands, notably this 'Chinese hat'. A sort of 'Jingling Johnnie', it has many bells and horsehair plumes which suggest an origin in Ottoman Turkey via the Austro-Hungarian empire.

(Above) A pioneer (*sapeur*) of the 1er RE, carrying the traditional felling axe. Unique features of this platoon include the full beard, and a leather apron. A pioneer section was a practical element of 19th century units; they helped clear the way for a marching column and carried out field engineering tasks. Their ceremonial potential on parade has been particularly exploited by the Legion since the run-up to the 1931 centenary.

(Left) During the time he spends at Aubagne for the signing of his contract of service, the future légionnaire is left alone for a time in the 1er RE's Salle d'Honneur or crypt. This houses the hand of Captain Danjou, laid-up colours, and a long roll of honour of Legion dead. Here the recruit has the opportunity to reflect on the fact that by signing his contract he places his life in the hands of the Legion, and must be ready to sacrifice it.

(Right) Far from being rushed into enlisting, every recruit for the highly selective Legion of today must go through several interviews. In cases where he does not speak good French the 1er RE can provide numerous interpreters in a large number of languages. Currently the Legion counts men of no less than 138 nationalities in its ranks; the current world situation is reflected in the fact that 65% of recent candidates have been from Eastern Europe and the Balkans. The average successful candidate is 23 years old, of a high physical standard, and his educational standard is statistically superior than that in the French army as a whole.

(Below)
The breast badge of the COM.LE

(Below) Men of the 1er RE in parade uniform for Camerone 1990. The Legion's distinctive features are the white képi, the green epaulettes fringed with red, a green necktie and a blue waist sash.

responsible for the Legion's famous central band, the Musique Principale.

The Foreign Legion Personnel Administration Company (CAPLE), some 70 strong, is responsible for the administration and transfer of papers of thousands of légionnaires each year who, while on courses, on short-duration postings, on leave or in transit, are not on the strength of any other unit. The CAPLE is also responsible for quartering the annual average of 5,400 volunteers attending the 14-day selection process.

Finally, the 80-strong Foreign Legion Transit Company (CTLE), based at Fort du Nogent near Paris, is responsible for the transfer of légionnaires to and from overseas postings.

The 1er RE also supplies the personnel for the Commandement de la Légion Étranger (COM.LE), with which it is closely interwoven. COM.LE forms the connecting link between the Legion and the French army command structure, and is headed by a Commandant – at the time of writing, Général de Division Piquemal – who is responsible for representing the interests of the Legion and all its members in contacts with the French army and defence ministry. COM.LE oversees all administration, personnel management, promotions and welfare matters, and regulates public works.

(Left) On arrival volunteers are given a short lecture about the Foreign Legion; they are told where the garrisons are located, what their future activities will be, and what the Legion expects of them.

(Below) The head of a company of the 1er RE march past the General Commandant of the Foreign Legion, their FAMAS assault rifles carried slung across their chests with bayonets fixed. The black képis with red crowns and gold or silver lace badges and distinctions mark out ranks from *sergent* (two gold sleeve chevrons) upwards as *sous-officiers*; the white képi is worn by the *hommes du rangs*, from *soldat de 2e classe* to *caporal-chef* (one gold above two green sleeve chevrons). The traditional fringed epaulettes and blue sash are not worn by warrant or commissioned officers.

Right) An *adjudant* (warrant officer) leads his platoon on parade on Camerone Day 1998. All wear the new service uniform, in the colour termed *'terre de France'*, which was introduced during the 1990s. (The summer version, with pale khaki shirt and 'French earth' trousers, is illustrated opposite and below.) Beneath the paratrooper's brevet on his right breast is the regimental badge of the 1er RE; on his left breast below his command brevet are the Médaille d'Outre-Mer (Overseas Medal) and Médaille de Defense Nationale. Although its tasks are basically administrative the 1er RE also provides specialist *compagnies de marche* for active service overseas, e.g. within the structure of the Division Daguet during the Gulf War of 1990-91.

(Below) Each year the Legion takes part in the parade in Paris to celebrate Bastille Day – the French national holiday; here the pioneers march past on 14 July 1998. Following tradition, the pioneers of the 1er RE lead the Legion contingent, followed by the Musique Principale – the only marching band in the parade – and by a rifle company. The Legion contingent forms the last element of foot troops in the parade, followed by the vehicles; this is because the légionnaires, with their traditional pace of 88 to the minute, march more slowly than the rest of the French infantry at 120 paces to the minute. The slow pace recalls that employed by the army as a whole before 1830, and is supposedly inherited from the largely-German Hohenlohe Regiment.

Operation Épervier: the Legion in Chad

On 11 August 1960 France granted independence to Chad – a poor, arid central African colony on the southern fringe of the Sahara, whose only wealth lay in its potential for mineral exploitation. Conflict between the ethnic Sudanese (black) and Arab elements of the mixed population was more or less inevitable. The first president, François Tombalbaye, was of Sudanese stock; his programme involved the formal division of the state along ethnic lines, and he quickly established a totalitarian regime which systematically oppressed the Muslim community. In 1966 the two largest opposition groups in Chad joined together in the Front de Liberation Nationale Tchadienne (FROLINA), and began to wage a guerrilla war against Tombalbaye, who still enjoyed French support.

In 1969 France sent the 2e REP and a Compagnie Motorisée de Légion Étrangère (CMLE) – a mixed company drawn from other Legion units – to support Tombalbaye. This was the Legion's first combat mission since the end of the Algerian War seven years before. Using helicopters and cross-country vehicles, the légionnaires were successful in a number of encounters with the rebels.

Forced onto the defensive, the rebel movement – which was supported by Libya and Algeria – fragmented into the Chad Liberation Front (FLT) and Chadian National Liberation Front (FROLINAT); later another faction, the 'Second Army', split off from FROLINAT. With Tombalbaye's position seemingly secured, the Legion was withdrawn in December 1971.

The president's rule was no wiser, however, and in 1975, following his imprisonment of several high-ranking figures, Tombalbaye was ousted by a military coup. The new head of state, Brigadier Felix Malloum, followed a policy of national reconciliation and managed to persuade most of the rebels to rally to the government. However, the Second Army – led by the formidable and ruthless intriguer Hisséne Habré, and supplied by Libya – remained in opposition, and from 1978 supported Libya's long-standing ambition to annexe the mineral-rich northern territories (the Aouzou Strip). Once again the Chadian government appealed to France for help.

From May 1978 to April 1980, as part of Operation Tacaud, elements of the 1er REC and 2e REI (with French air force support) operated successfully against Libyan-backed rebels; the 1er Escadron, 1er REC's AML 90 and AML 60

A sniper team armed with FR F-2 rifles, photographed during a halt for observation in the course of a reconnaissance patrol on the Chadian border by a unit of the 2e REI. Because the country is officially at peace a minimum of camouflage is used – French soldiers normally operate in such a way as to be recognisable at a distance so as to deter any insurgent from seeking trouble. When 'tactical' the snipers can, of course, merge into their surroundings completely, and are capable of accurate fire at ranges up to 800 yards.

(Left) A posting to Chad is very popular. The seemingly endless desert and savannah offer excellent training conditions and place great demands on légionnaires, particularly in such disciplines as navigation. There is an undeniable element of romance, however: here the modern légionnaire can feel closest to his forefathers in the old Mounted Companies of 90 years ago, and can experience for himself the desert adventures which otherwise exist only in novels. These men of the 2e REI's CCS were photographed during a navigation check; almost all légionnaires have a *chêche*, the traditional desert scarf which gives protection from sun and blowing sand.

(Below) The relationship between the Legion and the civilian population of Chad is generally good, and standing orders emphasise the 'hearts and minds' aspect of their mission. Here a 2e REI soldier gives medical aid to the inhabitants of one of the outlying villages which they visit during their weeks-long reconnaissance patrols along the northern border.

armoured cars saw action at Salal, Ati and Djedda. The Legion also provided security for French citizens in the capital, N'djamena, and set up and patrolled tolerated buffer zones between the various factions in this chronically volatile country. To provide this assistance while trying to remain aloof from the chaotic internal politics of Chad was not easy.

An apparent reconciliation between Malloum and Habré in 1979 proved short-lived; and in March 1980 fighting broke out again between government troops and Habré's newly formed Armed Forces of Northern Chad (FANT). After a period of more than usually confusing moves and counter-moves, which at one stage saw President Ghadaffi aiding the government against Habré, the FANT succeeded in defeating the government, and Habré set up a provisional council of state in 1982.

The largest deployment of French troops took place under Operation Manta, in response to an attempted annexation of the Aouzou Strip by Libyan army and FROLINAT forces in June 1983; this deployment included elements of the 1er REC and 2e REP. Libya's thrust was stopped on the 15th Parallel, which became the *de facto* border; and a period of tension on this 'Red Line' in 1984 brought elements of the 1er REC, 2e REP and 2e REI back to Chad with a watching brief, under Operation Épervier – the codename which still applies today to the French military presence.

After three years of relative peace the strengthened FANT

(government forces) launched an offensive northward with French support. French ground combat units were not involved, however, as the FANT alone achieved a decisive victory over Libyan armour in brigade strength at Wadi Doum and Bir Kora in March 1987, inflicting heavy casualties and driving Ghadaffi's forces back into Libya.

In 1990 Idris Debay became head of state, and since 1993 a transitional parliament has ruled Chad; but even since the conclusion of a peace treaty between the opposing sides in 1995 occasional battles still take place in northern Chad. Elements of the 1er REC, 2e REP, 2e REI and 6e REG have continued to rotate through Chad on regular postings throughout the 1990s.

The main task of the légionnaires, stationed today at Abéché, is patrolling the Chad/Libya border, where clashes still occur. However, the situation in the equally unstable Sudan (the former British protectorate to the east) has led to several serious border incursions by armed groups, and demands intensive surveillance of Chad's eastern frontier, too. The Legion also continues to provide security in N'djamena; in 1990 and 1992 the 2e REP companies on station had to respond to repeated acts of terrorism by assorted followers of Habré. The sappers of the 6e REG also fulfill the hazardous duty of helping to clear the countless mines, unexploded shells and other ordnance left scattered over this wasteland by 30 years of civil war.

(Above & below) When the 2e REI took over Camp Capitaine Crocci at Abéché from the marine paras of the 8e RPIMa in October 1989, they also inherited these two goats as mascots; and here they are paraded at the changing of the guard – a daily ceremony in all Legion garrisons. Note the left sleeve insignia of the goat handler. The seven-flame grenade on a black diamond with triple green edging identifies the Legion; above it, one gold above two green chevrons mark the rank of *caporal-chef*; and below it, three yellow chevrons record three completed five-year enlistments. By regulations, 20 years' service is the maximum term for a légionnaire; however, outstanding soldiers are treated indulgently in this matter.

(Left) Night vision equipment, as fitted to this légionnaire's 5.56mm FAMAS assault rifle, allows undetected night observation of an enemy, and night firing with a high probability of a first-time hit. The opposition are usually Chadian or Sudanese desert nomads, who lack such equipment. Their weapons are fairly modern and their knowledge of the terrain is good, but they are tactically primitive; even though armed with AK47s they persist in trying to fight in the open as if they were medieval spearmen. The helmet here is the standard M1978 F-1 type.

(Right) A sniper on duty in a guard post at the airport. The FR F-2 rifle resting on the sandbags is of 7.62mm calibre; since the introduction of the 'bullpup'-configured 5.56mm FAMAS as the standard personal weapon of the French infantryman, one qualified marksman per section has carried the longer-ranging, larger-calibre bolt-action rifle, with telescopic sight and bipod. Note the blue scarf tied around this légionnaire's left shoulder; this is the 1st Company's field identification sign. Individual 'rotating' companies or squadrons are usually posted to Chad rather than entire units.

(Left) Combat training in temperatures of 32°C (90°F) is an everyday occurence for légionnaires in Chad; in theory they must be able to delay any renewed Libyan invasion long enough for reinforcements to be flown in from France. Here, at the Zairois Pass – an important tactical feature on the southern approaches to Abéché – men of the 2e REI's 1er Cie. mount an attack under the covering fire of their section's sniper rifle, light machine gun and anti-armour rocket launcher.

17

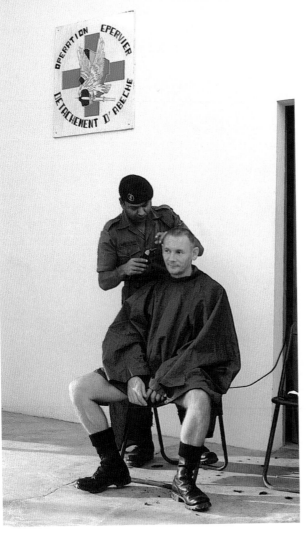

(Left) Whether on active service overseas or in a home garrison, personal cleanliness and keeping ones kit in good order are cornerstones of Legion discipline – and a regulation short haircut is an immediately visible sign of the required standards. In such far-flung postings as Abéché, in the absence of a specialist barber, the job is often performed by the medical personnel.

(Right) The Zairois Pass – the terrain of Chad offers opponents endless possibilities for an ambush, but defenders also enjoy plentiful cover.

(Left) In the more open savannah country of Chad longer-ranged weapons prove very effective. The French army still use the faithful old Browning M2HB .50 calibre heavy machine gun of World War II fame (and the British army have also decided in recent years to bring this classic weapon back out of storage). With a combat range of over 1,500m, it is effective even against light armoured targets at shorter distances.

(Below) Another classic infantry support weapon used by Legion units during their four-month tours in Chad is the 81mm mortar; a French design is the origin of this whole class of mortars, in use by all major armies since the 1930s-40s. The fire support platoon of each rifle company of an infantry regiment has two of these MO-81-LC Thomson-Brandt tubes. The total weight of 39.4kg – about 86.5lbs – breaks down into three man-loads; this portability is very useful in Chad's more mountainous regions.

(Above) Although a venerable design dating back 40 years to the Algerian War, the reliable belt-fed 7.5mm AA-52 general purpose machine gun was still in use here as the section light automatic support weapon; it has since been replaced by the Minimi (see page 69). It weighs 9.75kg – about 22lbs – and has a practical rate of fire of 200rpm; effective battle range is 800m, although maximum range is four times that distance. The round can penetrate 70cm (27.5ins) of wood or earth at 400 meters.

(Right) At the barracks gate the coat of arms of Operation Épervier – a sparrowhawk against the blue, yellow and red Chadian national colours – is displayed. This sentry is from the 2e REI, and the patch of the regiment's parent 6e Division Légère Blindée is just visible under the fringe of his parade epaulettes.

When the guard is turned out for inspection the trumpeter blows *'Au Caid'* ('To the chief', from the Arabic word). The unit commander then inspects the guard; he also asks his men if they have any worries or needs, which they may report directly to him on this occasion. On hearing the first notes of the trumpet call all other légionnaires must stand to attention, facing the gate, until it is over.

1er Régiment Étranger de Cavalerie

Stationed at Quartier Labouche in Orange, southern France, the 1er REC is today the only Legion cavalry regiment (a 2e REC existed briefly at the beginning of World War II, and again between 1946 and 1962). It is one of the two light armoured regiments of the 6e Division Légère Blindée, which represents an important part of France's Force d'Action Rapide (FAR) – 'Rapid Reaction Force'.

The current transformation of the French army into a smaller, all-volunteer force has already been mentioned. The divisional structure of the 6e DLB will not survive after 2002; but it will give birth to two armoured brigades with almost the same combined strength as the 6e DLB's current FAR mandate force. The 1er REC will continue to serve in this command.

The regiment was formed in Tunisia in 1921 with drafts from the 1er REI, French cavalry officers, and White Russian exiles. Between 1925 and 1934 the 1er REC saw active service in Syria, Algeria and Morocco, and performed security duties in North Africa thereafter. Elements of the regiment fought in France in 1940, in Tunisia in 1943, and – re-equipped with US materiel – in the landings in southern France in 1944; 1945 found the regiment, which served under the French 5th Armoured Division, in Germany, and it ended the war in Austria.

Between 1947 and 1954 the regiment served in Indochina, growing eventually to 17 squadrons for amphibious operations equipped with 'Crabs' and 'Alligators' (M29s and LVTs). The 1er REC fought in the Algerian War between 1954 and 1962, equipped with US M8 and later with French Panhard EBR F-11 armoured cars. It remained in the French concession areas of Algeria until October 1967, when it transferred to its present garrison.

The regiment has about 850 officers and men divided between a Command & Services Squadron (ECS); four sabre squadrons (1er, 2e, 3e, and 5e Escadrons); and an anti-tank squadron (4e Escadron). Each sabre squadron has four troops, each of three AMX 10RC heavy six-wheeled

(Top of page) Regimental breast and beret badges of the 1er REC, whose traditional colours are red, green and blue, and whose nickname is 'the Royal Foreigners'. In keeping with French cavalry practice the regiment's buttons, badges and lace are silver rather than gold.
(Below) The regiment's main weapon system is the AMX 10RC; its unstabilised 105mm

tank gun can fire HE, HEAT and APFSDS rounds out to a combat range of 2,000 meters. It is fitted for day and night fighting with a 360° panoramic periscope, thermal sight, laser range finder and fire direction computer. There is a crew of four – driver, gunner, loader and commander; and internal stowage for 38 x 105mm rounds and 4,000 rounds for the 7.62mm co-axial machine gun.

(Left) Peugeot motorcycles are used as liaison and scouting vehicles by all units of the Legion. This 1er REC despatch rider is on his way to squadron HQ with a reconnaissance report from an AMX 10RC crew operating under radio silence during an exercise.

(Right) As well as frequent operations in crisis-torn regions of Africa and the Middle East, the légionnaires of the 1er REC spend much of their time on exercises at national and international level. Here AMX 10RCs of the regiment disembark from a French navy landing craft during a FAR exercise involving elements of the French 6th Light Armoured, 9th Marine and 11th Parachute Divisions.

(Left) Légionnaires of the 1er REC and US Marines of 11 MEF often exercise together; here they practice precision firing with .50 calibre machine guns in the troop training area at Canjuers, Provence. As well as their armoured vehicles the Legion cavalry have a large number of these P4 light 4x4 vehicles fitted with the Browning M2HB. The P4 is a Peugeot modification of the Mercedes jeep; designated VLTT (for 'light all-terrain vehicle') by the French army, it is used as a weapons carrier, scout and liaison vehicle, and has a top speed of 108km/h (67 miles per hour).

(Opposite) A well-camouflaged P4 of the 1er REC during a FAR exercise in the Mediterranean area.

armoured cars. The 4e Escadron has 12 VAB armoured carriers fitted with HOT anti-tank missile launchers (and termed VCAC in this configuration). Additionally the 1er REC has at its disposal a number of lighter ERC 90 Sagaie armoured cars, with which it trains outstanding soldiers for detached duty with the 13e DBLE in Djibouti; however, these vehicles can also be pressed into regimental use to replace the heavy AMX 10RC at need, as in 1993 in Bosnia.

After operations in Chad from 1978 and in Beirut in 1983,

the 1990s began for the 1er REC with the regimental deployment to the Gulf under Operation Daguet. In 1992 the regiment provided a platoon of trained mechanised infantry for the French contingent to APRONUC in Cambodia. In 1993, to support the 2e REI – then serving with UNPROFOR in Sarajevo – the 1er REC sent a squadron equipped with the EBR 90 for a six-month tour in Bosnia.

This was followed by a second Bosnian tour in 1995 as part of BATINF 2; among other tasks, this involved taking up

positions on Mount Igman that May. As the situation intensified in June the 2e Esc. took its AMX 10RCs to Bosnia as part of the new quick-reaction force for the protection of UN troops, and occupied positions around Sarajevo (Operation Hermine). When UNPROFOR was replaced by IFOR – with a much more robust mandate for peace-making as well as peace-keeping, following the Dayton accords – the regiment's 3e Esc. was stationed in 1996 at Jablanica and Mostar, under Multi-National Division South-West (Operation Salamandre). At the end of that year followed Operation Almandine II, and in 1997 Operation Pelican II, in the Central African Republic and Congo-Brazzaville.

(Right) The 16-ton AMX 10RC is powered by a Boudouin diesel giving a top speed of 85km/h (52.8mph) and a range with full tanks of 1,000km (620 miles). It has a hydraulically adjustable ground clearance of between 0.2 and 0.6m (0.65 to 1.9ft); this can also be used to raise or lower the vehicle at left, right, front or back to distribute the weight for obstacle crossing. The AMX 10RC can cross a trench 1.65m (5.4ft) wide and climb vertical obstacles 0.8m (2.6ft) high.

(Opposite) The AMX 10RC is prepared for water crossing by setting up a swimming vane, made with clear plastic panels to give the driver an uninterrupted view. It is propelled by two turbines at left and right of the stern, giving a top speed in water of 7km/h (4.35 miles per hour).

Operation Daguet: the Legion in the Gulf War

On 2 August 1990 the armed forces of the Iraqi dictator Saddam Hussein invaded the sovereign state of Kuwait – one of the wealthiest of the Persian Gulf oil sheikdoms – and annexed it as the 19th province of Iraq, in pursuit of a long-standing claim. The invasion was immediately condemned by the United Nations, which passed a number of resolutions calling for Iraqi withdrawal and imposing sanctions. Finally, by Resolution 678, the UNO empowered a coalition of 29 states – led by the USA, Great Britain and France, but also including a number of Arab nations – to expel Iraqi forces from Kuwait by force from 15 January 1991.

By 7 August 1990 the USA had already begun the transfer of forces to Saudi Arabia under Operation Desert Shield, followed within days by Britain and at the end of September by France. The French government's original stance was that French troops would only help defend Saudi Arabia and would not take part in any future offensive operations; but public opinion soon persuaded the National Assembly to authorise full participation in Coalition operations to liberate Kuwait. By the time the air war opened on 17 January 1991 some 600,000 Coalition troops were in theatre, facing a theoretical total of about 530,000 Iraqi forces.

The first French formation sent to the Gulf was the 6th Light Armoured Division (6e DLB). On 30 September the 2e Cie., 2e REI and 1er Esc., 1er REC landed at the Saudi port of Yanbu, which would remain the French rear logistic base. The French operation was codenamed Daguet, and the tactical formation assembled in country, Division Daguet. During the weeks which followed the remainder of the 2e REI and the 1er REC arrived, together with the 6e REG and a 'marching company' of the 1er RE. Shortly before the fighting started a deep reconnaissance and action group was formed which included the Deep Recce & Action Commando from the 2e REP. For the first time since the Algerian War more than 2,500 légionnaires were operating together.

The other main combat assets of General Janvier's Division Daguet were: part 1er Régiment de Hussards Parachutistes (1er RHP), light recce; 13e Dragons Parachutistes (13e RDP), light recce; 1er Spahis (1er RS), recce; part Régiment d'Infanterie-Chars de Marine (RICM), recce;

(Below) VAB armoured infantry carriers of the 2e REI at the French disembarkation port of Yanbu. Ahead of them lay a desert march of more than 1,200 miles, which had to be planned to avoid passing through the holy city of Medina – the presence of non-Muslim troops was a contentious issue in Saudi Arabia. The journey was a punishing test for the VAB, which proved itself highly reliable despite the fine, penetrating sand.

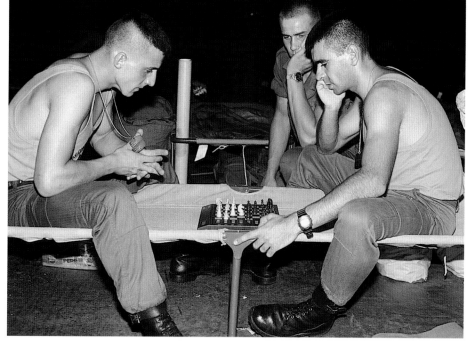

(Right) Waiting – the traditional occupation of soldiers. Here légionnaires of the 2e REI pass the time with a game of chess in the oven-like tented accomodation at Yanbu.

(Below right) This soldier of the 2e REI is of Moroccan origin. His fluency in Arabic was useful for communicating with the local Saudi population, and later in the interrogation of Iraqi prisoners. The Division Daguet took the surrender of 2,956 Iraqi troops, about 1,000 of them during the first 24 hours of the advance on As-Salman.

3e Infanterie de Marine (3e RIMa), mechanised; part 21e RIMa, mechanised; part 1er Infanterie (1er RI), anti-tank; 4e Dragons (4e RD), tanks; 503e Chars de Combat (503e RCC), tanks; AA battery, 35e Régiment d'Artillerie Parachutiste (35e RAP); 11e Artillerie de Marine (11e RAMa); and the 3e and 5e Régiments d'Hélicoptères de Combat (3e & 5e RHC). These were backed up by the usual support and services units, giving the division a total strength of around 12,500 men with 40 x AMX 30B2 main battle tanks, 120 x AMX 10RC heavy armoured cars, 250 x VAB armoured carriers, 12 x ERC 90 Sagaie armoured cars, 18 x towed 155mm howitzers, about 124 Gazelle and Puma helicopters, and some 3,000 miscellaneous vehicles.

On 4 October, after a 2,000km (1,250 mile) march through the desert, the advance guard of the French contingent under the Legion's Lieutenant-Colonel Lecerf reached – according to their GPS satellite location systems – Arenas, a completely featureless spot in the desert east of Hafar-al-Batin. Some 60km (37 miles) to the north of them were the Iraqis; to the east was an Egyptian division; to the west a pair of Saudi Arabian bedouin stood guard. In this godforsaken place the French prepared to face any Iraqi attack which might materialise. Between the Iraqi army and Riadh, capital of Saudi Arabia, stood only the Division Daguet, an Egyptian and a Syrian division and a handful of Saudi Arabian brigades; and the French were very conscious that since the bulk of the Coalition forces were at that time concentrated on the Gulf coast, the Iraqis could easily have struck around the desert flank. During the period October-December more and more Coalition reinforcements arrived, and the division had more time for training and adapting to the extreme desert climate.

The air war began at 0100 hours on 17 January 1991 with massive Coalition air attacks on strategic targets all over Kuwait and Iraq. An hour later the Division Daguet was on the march from Hafar-al-Batin, some 300km (185 miles) west to Al-Rafah; because of a SCUD (Iraqi missile) alert the move was carried out under full NBC protection. During the four-week air offensive the division remained on combat readiness. In mid-February, a few days before the beginning of the ground war, an Iraqi vehicle patrol trying to reconnoitre the Al-Rafah area was spotted by légionnaires of the 2e REI, who called down artillery fire. The 11e RAMa fired its first shots in anger since the Algerian War, dropping 123 155mm shells on the given co-ordinates.

On 22 February elements of the 2e REI and 6e REG penetrated 5km into Iraq to take out an enemy position codenamed 'Nachez' which dominated the division's planned route of advance up an escarpment; on the 23rd sappers of the 6e REG and their American counterparts worked to prepare the ground; and on the 24th the Coalition stormed forward. The French mission was codenamed 'Princess of Cleves'; they would operate with the US 82nd Airborne Division on the extreme left of the allied advance, where their heavy wheeled vehicles were suited for rapid flanking manoeuvres.

On the night of the 24th they climbed the frontier escarpment without opposition, and began their deep strike into Iraqi territory. They pushed forward on two axes: on the concrete road the 'Texas Axis' consisted of the US 82nd and the French Marines; the desert 'Beaulieu Axis' was followed by the GMLE (Foreign Legion Marching Group) of the 1er REC and 2e REI;

(Main photo) The long wait before the start of the ground offensive was not wasted. As soon as the arrival of reinforcements reduced any immediate threat of an Iraqi attack into the French defence sector in the Saudi desert, Divison Daguet began a punishing cycle of training in desert warfare tactics. Here légionnaires deploy after leaving their VABs, with the support of the 12.7mm (.50cal) heavy machine gun mounted on each carrier, and one of the two 20mm 53T2 cannon of the fire support platoon. The temperature is around 45°C (113°F); the burning sand and stones stretch to the horizon in all directions, as flat as a table. Here, if anywhere on earth, the young légionnaires should feel in touch with their forefathers.

(Inset) Men of the 2e Cie., 2e REI watch their VABs disembarking at Yanbu.

the 6e REG was divided to provide an engineer spearhead for both columns. Their objective was the town and airfield of As-Salman. In their path stood the Iraqi General Zabidi's 45th Infantry Division, 8,000 strong, equipped mainly with Russian materiel but also with some Chinese T-59 tanks.

In just three days the allies covered the 150km (95 miles) to As-Salman, breaking through a Soviet-style Iraqi defence position – codenamed 'Rochambeau' – on a wide front. This was so thoroughly degraded by air attack, MLRS and artillery that the Iraqi troops offered little resistance to the Coalition force. This opened the way to As-Salman and the Euphrates river. The 1er REC and 2e REI carried out a frontal attack on the airfield; here the 1er REC's 4e Escadron engaged

with their VCAC/HOT for the first time, against Iraqi AA artillery positions which had opened up with 14.5mm heavy machine guns and 23mm cannons. By the morning of 25 February the French troops were able to consolidate defensive positions to protect the potentially vulnerable flank of the Coalition thrust into Kuwait.

On the 27th the liberation of Kuwait was accomplished and a truce was concluded; on 3 March the armistice negotiations began. For the French the campaign ended at As-Salman – except for the sappers of the 6e REG, who remained to help clear mines in Kuwait and Iraq. It was while carrying out this mission that the Legion suffered their only fatality, when Adjudant-Chef Sudre fell victim to an Iraqi mine.

(Left) An AMX 10RC commander of 1er Esc., 1er REC in the desert around Hafar-al-Batin. Two of the main aspects of training during the autumn and winter of 1990 were NBC precautions – at a time when the threat of Iraqi SCUDs had to be taken very seriously; and desert navigation. The utter lack of landmarks and the unchanging similarity of vast regions of desert pose difficulties even in the age of GPS satellite positioning, since not all the French vehicles had this equipment.

(Below left) The AMX 10RC which the 'Royal Foreigners' ride into battle is, in effect, a wheeled tank. Its 105mm gun is shared with main battle tanks, and even in 1991 its fire control systems were relatively sophisticated, making it a match for the older Iraqi armour by day or night. During the ground fighting the Division Daguet's armoured regiments fired a total of 560 rounds of 105mm at Iraqi targets.

(Below right) A convoy of VABs and trucks halt during a desert march. Each rifle platoon has three VABs, each carrying a squad of eight to ten men; versions of the VAB are also used for command vehicles, heavy weapons carriers, and so forth. The 4x4 VAB is amphibious, has night vision equipment, mounts a .50cal heavy machine gun, and has eight firing ports in the hull sides.

(Right) Each of the 2e REI's four rifle companies has it own fire support platoon, with two each 81mm mortars, 20mm cannon and MILAN ATGW launchers. Here the MILAN section of the 2e Cie. practices acquiring a target; this battle-proven anti-tank guided weapon is effective at ranges between 25 and 2,500m by day and night when fitted with MIRA heat-imaging sights. During the ground combat phase of Desert Storm the infantry of the French division fired 22 MILANs at enemy vehicles and positions.

(Left) Légionnaires of a MILAN team of 2e Cie., 2e REI; the firing post weighs 17kg (37.5lbs), and the packed missile 13kg (28.6lbs). Nearly all the légionnaires seem to have acquired the traditional *chêche* sun-and-sand scarf, which is both practical and dashing in appearance – and therefore popular.

29

(Above) The 2e REI is unique among French mechanised infantry units in having two integral heavy mortar platoons – 12 x Hotchkiss-Brandt 120mm MO-120-RT61 tubes on wheeled carriages, instead of the usual six – within the regimental Recce & Support Company (CEA). This gives the unit considerable punch, almost equivalent to having its own light artillery.

(Above right) An officer of the 2e REI in an HQ tent – not standard French Army issue, but presented to the unit by the Saudi Arabians. In the background is the company *fanion*; and the wall is decorated with one of the Legion's traditional 'family portraits' – that of General Paul Rollet, 'Father of the Legion', who became the Legion's first Inspector in 1931.

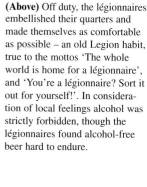

(Above) Off duty, the légionnaires embellished their quarters and made themselves as comfortable as possible – an old Legion habit, true to the mottos 'The whole world is home for a légionnaire', and 'You're a légionnaire? Sort it out for yourself!'. In consideration of local feelings alcohol was strictly forbidden, though the légionnaires found alcohol-free beer hard to endure.

(Below) The VAB in its anti-tank guided weapon configuration. The VCAC/HOTs of 4e Esc., 1er REC had their baptism of fire at As-Salman, destroying several Iraqi gun positions. The Euro-missile Mephisto system, with 360° traverse, fires four HOT out to ranges of 4,000m; another eight are stowed in the carrier, and the launcher can be lowered for reloading under armoured protection. The vehicle has a crew of four.

(Left) The tip of the spearhead in the push along the Texas Axis was a VAB and a squad of 6e REG sappers led by Adjudant Kjan. They took some 50 prisoners, many of whom seemed only too glad to surrender, and a large number of weapons. The légionnaires wore NBC suits and splinter-proof body armour – a torture when training in the full heat of the Saudi desert, but less so during the cold winter nights of the February advance.

(Right) Amongst other vehicles, units of the Division Daguet destroyed 20 T-55 (or Chinese T-59) and T-62 main battle tanks, 17 light armoured vehicles and 114 'soft skinned' wheeled vehicles of the Iraqi forces; 26 artillery pieces were also destroyed. Two T-72 tanks, 40 artillery pieces and 70 mortars of between 82mm and 120mm calibre were captured.

(Right) Homecoming – on their way back to their bases units of the Division Daguet disembarked at Toulon. Thousands of onlookers thronged the decorated streets of the old naval port city to welcome the troops home; here the VABs pass in parade, still in their desert warpaint but with the clutter of campaign stowage cleared away.

2e Régiment Étranger d'Infanterie

The 2e Régiment Étranger was born in Algeria in 1841, when the number of foreign battalions had increased to six and it was decided to divide the Foreign Legion into two units. This was a period of major fighting against the great Algerian leader Abd-el-Kader – of savage assaults, desperate sieges and exhausting marches. The Legion would continue to be employed vigorously by the able and far-sighted new French commander, General Bugeaud – an advocate of fast-moving light columns. The 1er RE was then based around Algiers, and the 2e RE at Bône.

The two regiments were once again amalgamated in 1862, but the 2e RE was reborn in 1885, based at Saida. Men of the regiment contributed to the drafts for French West Africa, Tonkin, Dahomey and Madagascar. For the long Moroccan campaign in 1900-1918 the 2e – like the 1er – provided both rifle battalions and mule-mounted mobile infantry companies – crack units which covered extraordinary distances. The regiment contributed thousands of men to the 'marching regiments' of World War I; and returned to Morocco in 1920, reorganised as the 2e REI. Headquartered at Meknès, it fought in many campaigns until the final pacification of Morocco in 1934.

Disbanded in 1943, its effectives transferred to other units, it was reborn at the end of World War II and shipped immediately to Annam (South Vietnam). Its battalions fought all over Vietnam throughout the Indochina War, the 1st Battalion being almost completely destroyed at Dien Bien Phu in May 1954. In 1955 the 2e REI was back in Algeria; it fought through most of the Algerian War as a motorised intervention unit in the south-west – the Moroccan border country where its mule-borne forefathers of the Mounted

(Top of page) Regimental breast and beret badges of the 2e REI; the horseshoe recalls the old mule-borne Mounted Companies, which operated with such success on the Algerian/Moroccan border in the days of the great General Lyautey before, during and after World War I.

(Below) VAB of the 2e REI disembarking from a French navy landing craft during Exercise Tramontana 94 on the Mediterranean coast. Amphibious training plays a large part in FAR exercises, since deployment outside Europe is always possible, and the heavy armour must go by sea even if the personnel can be flown in. Note the 12.7mm (.50cal) machine gun mounted on the commander's hatch, and the side hatches allowing the infantry squad to use their personal weapons on the move, if feasible.

Companies had made their name 60 years before. After Algerian independence the 2e REI was one of the French units which stayed on until 1968 in remote Saharan bases; it was disbanded that January, the last Legion unit to leave Algeria.

Reformed in Corsica in 1972 as the 2e RE, it pursued a combination training and operational role: a headquarters and three rifle companies formed the air-transportable GOLE (Foreign Legion Operational Group), while the rest of the regiment formed GILE (Foreign Legion Instruction Group), performing the functions that were later taken over by the 4e RE. It provided men for Djibouti in 1976, Chad in 1978-79, and the UN force in Beirut, Lebanon, in 1983. The 2e had become 'Foreign Infantry' once more in June 1980; it has since provided the French army's strongest mechanised infantry unit, and a major asset of the Rapid Reaction Force. At the time of writing there are reports that it will soon be enlarged even further, to eight companies including a permanent Rear Base Company, and that it will take responsibility for trials of all new infantry equipment.

The 1990s opened for the 2e REI with the Gulf War, followed by the provision of personnel to the UN mission in Cambodia and, in larger numbers, to UNPROFOR in Bosnia. Strong elements were shipped to that country in 1995 to help establish a security zone round Sarajevo. In 1996 the 3e Cie. rotated to Bosnia under Operation Salamandre, while 200

(Above) One of the techniques which figures prominently in 2e REI training is the destruction of enemy tanks in built-up areas. Because their main armament can only be used to a fraction of its potential in such a scenario, tanks are particularly vulnerable during street fighting (as recent events in the Chechen city of Grozny have reminded us). As well as the long-range MILAN wire-guided system the légionnaires also have available to them the 89mm LRAC (Lance-Rocket Anti-Char) with an effective range of 600m, and the 120mm RAC APILAS, with a range of 300 metres. Bringing these weapons into action, with accuracy and while remaining unobserved, demands a high degree of training.

(Right) 'The artillery of captains' – as well as the very heavy 120mm mortars of the CEA, the rifle companies have the support of their own pairs of 81mm tubes, offering high-angle indirect fire against enemy positions invisible to the infantry's direct fire weapons. The MO-81-LC has a range of 5,000m, and fires high explosive, illumination and smoke bombs; the HE rounds can be fused for impact, proximity or time delay. The three-man crew carry the mortar broken down into three loads – baseplate, tube, and bipod with optics – and each man also carries two bombs; the remainder of the immediate use ammunition is divided between the rest of the section. Mortarmen of the 2e REI are expected to fire 15 rounds a minute.

men were attached to Operation Almandine in the Central African Republic. That November the whole 2e REI were transferred to the area around Sarajevo as BATINF 6, under IFOR and finally SFOR. In 1997 the 4e Cie. participated in Operation Pélican II at Brazzaville in the Congo.

Stationed at the Quartier Vallongue in Nîmes, southern France, the 1,200 officers and men of the 2e REI are divided between the Command & Services Company (CCS); Reconnaissance & Support Company (CEA); and four rifle companies (1er, 2e, 3e and 4e Compagnies de Combat). The CEA, the strongest of its kind in the French army, has three anti-tank platoons with a total of 24 MILAN ATGW posts; two mortar platoons with a total of 12 x 120mm mortars; two automatic cannon platoons with a total of ten 20mm electrically-operated single-barrel weapons; and two recce platoons with VBL and VLTT P4 vehicles. The unit has a total of 92 VABs used as troop carriers, command, MILAN and mortar vehicles.

Each rifle company consists of a command group and four platoons. Each platoon has three squads, each currently ten men strong, mounted in a VAB carrier and armed with the FAMAS rifle, FR-F2 sniping rifle, Minimi light machine gun and LRAC 89mm rocket launcher; at need the 120mm APILAS anti-armour weapon is also available. Each company also has two 81mm mortars and two MILAN posts, and two 20mm cannon from the CEA may be attached.

As well as Camerone, the regiment also celebrates 2 September each year – the anniversary of the battle of El-Moungar in 1903. There Captain Vauchez's 2e RE Mounted Company, ambushed by large numbers of Doui Menia tribesmen while escorting a convoy in the far southern Algerian/Moroccan border country, resisted for eight hours; of 115 all ranks 33 légionnaires, including both officers, were killed, and a further 40 wounded. The 2e REI has today the strongest attachment to the traditions of the old Mounted Companies, and the regimental mascot is a mule.

(Above) All modern troops have to be trained to march, dig, and operate their weapons while wearing NBC protection. This is stiflingly hot and uncomfortable, and inevitably degrades vision and hearing badly – but it has to be done. Here men of a fire support platoon of the CEA watch the 'fall of shot' of their devastating 20mm electrically-operated cannon.

(Right) The 2.3kg (5lb) projectile of the 89mm LRAC will penetrate up to 400mm (15.7ins) of conventional steel armour at up to 600m range, and is thus deadly to all of the world's armoured fighting vehicles except the latest models of main battle tank protected by sophisticated steel/ceramic composite armours. A crew of two men carry the 4.8kg (10.5lb) launcher tube and its ammunition.

(Left) The basic troop-carrier version of the VAB is designated VTT. It accomodates a driver, commander, and ten fully equipped infantrymen. This 4 x 4 amphibious vehicle weighs 10.3 tons, has a load capacity of 2.8 tons, can reach a maximum road speed of 92km/h (57mph) and a water speed of 7km/h (4.3 miles per hour). It is powered by a Renault 6-cylinder turbo-diesel engine, and has a range of 1,000m (620 miles) on a 300-litre (66-gal) tank of fuel.

(Below) Men of an anti-tank squad of the 2e REI on their way to their position during Exercise Dragon Hammer 90. As well as their personal FAMAS rifles they carry (foreground) the 89mm LRAC and (background) the 120mm APILAS.

(Left) Co-operation with other nations in exercises and operations has been a frequent experience for the légionnaire of the 1990s. Here a 2e REI soldier – displaying the 6e DLB shoulder patch on his drab green F-1 fatigues – chats to a US Marine of 11 Marine Expeditionary Force.

Together with the 2e REP, the 2e REI helps form the spearhead of France's Rapid Reaction Force, and must be ready for deployment at short notice anywhere in the world, on a broad range of missions. Its strength, mobility and integral firepower fit it for any task, from hostage rescue to conventional combat, in any type of terrain.

(Below) The regimental flag of the 2e REI is paraded. The colour party consists of an officer flag-bearer flanked by two senior NCOs and followed by three junior ranks. Apart from their black (officially, midnight blue) and red képis with gold lace, chinstraps and badges, senior NCOs have gold threads mixed into the red crescents and fringes of their *epaulettes de tradition*. The 2e REI boasts the battle honours Sébastopol 1855, Kabylie 1857, Magenta 1859, Camerone 1863 (all Legion units bear this honour), Extrême-Orient 1884-1885, Dahomey 1892, Madagascar 1898-1905; Maroc 1907, 1913, 1921, 1934; and Indochine 1946-1954. The flag is decorated with the Croix de Guerre TOE ('for external theatres of operations') with two palms, the City of Milan Commemorative Medal, and the pale blue and red lanyard of the Croix de Guerre TOE.

(Above) The training of the légionnaire is made as realistic and challenging as possible, and he is often faced with different combat scenarios in rapid succession, to encourage initiative. During this combat firing exercise the crew of a 20mm cannon of the regiment's CEA have just heard the NBC alarm, and are scrambling into their protective equipment.

(Right) VAB VTTs of the 3e Cie., 2e REI – identifiable from rather closer up by the tactical markings on the front. There are a total of five roof hatches; all five open to the front, thus giving the soldiers a certain amount of protection against splinters and infantry weapons. The commander's heavy machine gun mounting also has armour protection.

Although today's légionnaire is often carried into battle in VABs or Puma helicopters, he is still trained to make long, punishing cross-country marches on foot, marching and running with weapons and heavy packs. High levels of fitness and endurance are demanded of all ranks.

UNPROFOR, IFOR and SFOR: the Legion in Former Yugoslavia

The collapse of the Federal People's Republic of Yugoslavia began in 1980 with the death of President Tito. That ruthless but far-sighted leader had imposed peaceful, if grudging co-operation on the many and geographically intermingled groups within his multinational state. His successors failed to rule with sufficient even-handedness. Simmering communal resentments – born of foreign occupations, rebellions, collaborations, religious hatreds and a tradition of blood-feud, stretching from the medieval Turkish invasions up to the aftermath of World War II – boiled up again during the 1980s. The Serbian President Milosevic encouraged these communal hostilities for his own short-term ends; and in June 1991 Slovenia and Croatia each declared their unilateral independence.

The Slovenes, with a unified population and a less tangled history, successfully resisted an attack by the Serb-dominated Yugoslavian army (JVA), and have since managed to remain aloof from the bloodbath. But in Croatia the Serbian minority in the Krajina area resisted secession, and civil war broke out in this border region. In October 1991 Bosnia-Herzogovina, a very mixed and traditionally tolerant province, also declared its independence; here too Serbian-populated areas rose against the new entity, founding their 'Republic of Srpska' with support from Belgrade.

In February 1992 general civil war broke out in Bosnia and its surrounding borderlands, involving a bewildering number of factions. At first the Serbs, supported by the JVA, achieved considerable success against Croatia and the Bosnian Muslims, the more so since in April 1993 the Muslim and Croatian Bosnians also started fighting each other. After they joined forces in a grudging but pragmatic federation in March 1994 they began to inflict severe defeats on the Serbs. In the savage tradition of the Balkans, the fighting was characterised by widespread atrocities against civilians, who also suffered badly from hunger and the breakdown of medical services as refugees fled the fighting.

Eventually international public opinion became sickened by the spectacle, and from April 1992 UN troops were sent into Bosnia – but with a mandate limited to monitoring various short-lived local ceasefires and safeguarding the delivery of humanitarian aid. By 1995, against a background of escalating fighting, this UNPROFOR presence was being ignored or manipulated, largely for Serbian interests: UN convoys and bases were shot up, personnel were taken hostage, and UN units had to stand aside while large-scale massacres were committed almost before their eyes. This intolerable situation led to the creation of a UN Rapid Reaction Force from British and French units in Bosnia. With limited NATO air

(Below) Sarajevo airport was the UN logistic base and depot throughout the Bosnian war. Safeguarding the UN installations all over the area was hampered by the fact that the only link between the besieged city and Bosnian positions to the south-west lay either across the airport or through a tunnel beneath it. All supplies and reinforcements for the Bosnian troops in the city had to pass this way – which naturally attracted constant and heavy Serbian fire. Photographed in February 1992, légionnaires of the 2e REP watch Bosnian troop movements in the ruined suburb of Butmir.

support, this force relieved the Serbian siege of Sarajevo in spring 1995 – a first step towards a more robust attempt to at least limit the horrors of the Bosnian conflict.

In November 1995, under strong UN and NATO pressure, the temporarily exhausted Serbs and the Bosnian Muslim/ Croatian federation accepted the Dayton peace accords. These were to be enforced by the Peace Implementation Force (IFOR), which consisted of troops from all NATO and 19 non-NAT0 countries. In 1996 IFOR's mandate was extended indefinitely, and it was retitled Stabilisation Force (SFOR).

Legion deployments

Since the first UN presence in April 1992 French units have made an important contribution in Bosnia, taking part in all UN and NATO operations. The first Legion contingent was from the 2e REP; the 1er and 4e Cies., part of the CCS and CEA, and a tactical headquarters under Colonel Poulet arrived in Sarajevo in December 1992-January 1993. Their mission was to secure the airport for UNPROFOR use, to escort aid convoys and to supervise aid distribution in the area. At the end of February, Légionnaire Benko of 1er/2e REP became the first fatality and two other men were injured when mortar fire struck the vehicle park.

In June 1993 the paras of the 2e REP were relieved by the 1er and 3e Cies. and CCS of the 2e REI under Colonel de Richoufftz, supported by a squadron of ERC 90 Sagaie armoured cars from the 1er REC. During their six-month tour the légionnaires of the 1er/2e REI, with help from 6e REG sappers, established a new post at Hadzici east of Sarajevo to control the so-called 'Log Track'; this involved filling 13,000 sandbags in 13 days. The post, operational on 15 August 1993, was held by 28 men with a 20mm cannon, the 12.7mm machine guns mounted on their three VABs, and two MILAN

(Above right) Their duties often took the paras of the 2e REP into Sarajevo city itself, e.g. when escorting VIPs to negotiations with the warring factions. Their vehicles were shot at with monotonous regularity on 'Sniper Alley', the main road in from the airport.

(Right) February 1993 – from the machine gun cupola of a VAB-VTT a 2e REP légionnaire watches a UN Antonov 26 shuttle plane taking off from Sarajevo airport. These aircraft often came under Serbian machine gun fire – as did the conspicuous white vehicles of UNPROFOR troops.

(Above) A humanitarian aid convoy passes the gate guard at Sarajevo airport.

(Below) One of the tasks of the légionnaires was escorting aid convoys through battle zones. They were often hindered by Serbian police or militia checkpoints. These unwelcome halts could last hours, or several days, while intensive negotiations took place. Meanwhile the soldiers of the escort, operating under difficult rules of engagement, had to try to prevent theft from the vehicles.

ATGW firing posts. Légionnaires also manned an OP at Bjelasnica; and defended positions on Mount Igman against frequent Serbian attempts to retake this strategic point dominating the supply route into Sarajevo.

In 1995 the 2e REP returned as part of the French Brigade Balbuzard which, together with elements of the British 24 Airmobile Brigade, represented the reserve of the new Rapid Reaction Force set up by UNPROFOR that June. In the same month Colonel Lecerf's 2e REI led the RRF's Task Force Alpha into action to break the siege ring around Sarajevo. On 8 June the unit's 120mm mortars and their crews were lifted from the transport ship *La Foudre* off the Adriatic coast, and flown into BAT 5's position on Mount Igman – to be greeted, luckily without casualties, by Serbian shellfire. On 23 June the remainder of the 2e REI, supported by 2e/1er REC, were landed at Ploce. After intensive joint training the task force became operational on 23 July 1995; they transferred to Mount Igman after a spate of attacks on aid convoys and UN positions in Sarajevo, in which two French officers had been killed. TF Alpha consisted of the 2e Cie. and the CEA from 2e REI, the 1er REC squadron, and elements of the 6e REG; TF Bravo was drawn from the British Devonshire & Dorset Regiment with Warrior IFVs, two 105mm gun batteries from 19 Regiment Royal Artillery, and armoured engineers.

The Serbs were given a deadline to remove their heavy weapons from a protection zone around Sarajevo; they ignored it, and on 29 August Operation Vulcan opened with a three-hour attack on AA and mortar positions, bunkers and a munitions factory by 60 NATO aircraft and RRF artillery. On 12 September, after two weeks of such attacks, the Serbs complied with the UN ultimatum. Three days later the first aid flights and convoys reached the beleagured city.

Autumn 1995 saw the 2e REP guarding the artillery positions on Mount Igman; and on 20 December the unit came under the transfer of authority from UNPROFOR to IFOR. Together with the 3e/1er REC, the Legion paras served with the new French-led Multi-National Division South-West, and until April 1996 they patrolled stretches of the 'inter-ethnic borderline' (IEBL). They dismantled unauthorised control posts, supervised the withdrawal of heavy weapons, inventoried the ordnance of the warring factions – and brought humanitarian aid to civilian populations ground down by five long years of atrocious civil war. During this Operation Salamandre they suffered from the harsh weather conditions: in February 1996 the 2e REP's camp at Vrapcici was completely devastated when the river Neretva broke its banks – the flood was violent enough to wash away even VABs.

Three companies of the 6e REG had already assisted the French UN battalions BATINF 2 and 4 at Sarajevo, and the 2e Cie. had formed part of Operation Hermine by the RRF. In February 1996 the whole regiment was transferred for four months to Rajlovac north-east of Sarajevo to serve as the divisional engineer unit (BATGEN); their first task was clearing mines and other ordnance from this former Serbian air force school, then restoring water and electricity supplies.

They then spread out to perform the same tasks in the surrounding area, as well as rebuilding bridges and carrying out other repair work for the population.

The most recent Legion deployment to Bosnia at the time of writing began for the 2e REI in November 1997, when it arrived for a six-month tour at Rajlovac under SFOR's Franco-German Brigade.

(Right) During the 2e REP's time with UNPROFOR the regiment's VBL vehicle was nicknamed the 'Sarajevo Taxi', because it was so often used to take officers and VIPs under armoured protection to and from the city or to the HQ of UN troops in Bosnia at Kiseljak. Behind the vehicle is the airport control tower.

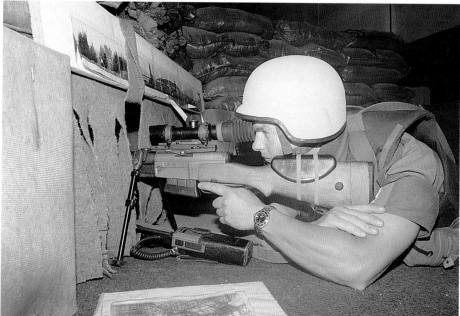

(Left) Serbian snipers in sky-scrapers in southern Sarajevo were a long-standing scourge, murdering large numbers of civilians and often firing on UN troops. In 1992 the 2e REP installed counter-snipers to return fire; they often came to know well the enemy's favoured positions, habits and patterns of relief. A panoramic view of the city is taped above this sniper's loophole. With the new IFOR mandate this campaign against snipers could be pursued with much greater rigour – the légionnaires no longer had to wait until they were fired upon themselves. Super-heavy .50cal American sniper rifles also supplemented this standard FR-F2.

(Left) This 2e REP squad sniper oversees the distribution of aid supplies in the suburb of Butmir. Like soldiers everywhere, the légionnaires always got on well with the local children, and often gave them sweets collected together from their ration packs.

(Above left) No more blue helmets or white vehicles... Protected by a Spectra ballistic helmet and splinter-proof body armour, this sniper of the 2e REI is operating with the British gunners of 19 Regiment RA on Mount Igman. The French and British task forces of the Rapid Reaction Force together comprised Multi-National Brigade Aquila. Note the 'LEGION ETRANGERE' title on the national brassard worn for multi-national operations.

(Above right) The state-of-the-art vision and fire control equipment of the artillery observation teams and platoon officers allowed the return of any hostile fire by night as well as by day. Here a 2e REI mortarman lays his 120mm tube on a new target.

(Below) The 2e REI mortar platoons on Mount Igman often engaged the firing positions of the Serbs besieging Sarajevo. After one Serbian mortar attack on French troops in the city on 22 July 1995, one six-tube 120mm platoon dropped 90 rounds on the enemy within a few moments. There were no further attacks on UN troops from that position.

(Right) An essential task for the IFOR contingents was the checking of the warring factions' ordnance depots and the destruction of materiel which violated the terms of the Dayton peace accords. Here, in March 1996, a Legion sapper of 3e Cie., 6e REG examines improvised mortar bombs illegally stored in a cellar in Sarajevo. During its six-month tour as BATGEN of Multi-National Division South-West the 6e REG blew up tons of ammunition, weapons and equipment and lifted a huge number of mines.

(Below) August 1995 – from a position in the woods on Mount Igman the crew of an AMX 10RC of the 1er REC observe the region around Hadzici, a suburb of Sarajevo. Together with NATO air attacks and RRF artillery fire, the presence of French and British armoured units on Igman was a major factor in persuading the Serbs to loosen the siege and withdraw their heavy weapons. Had they not done so, a RRF ground operation was planned and would have been launched at short notice. (*Sergent* Ralph Gunther, who was killed by Serbian snipers while accompanying an aid convoy in 1994, had been a member of the crew of this particular vehicle.)

(Left) On a road on Mount Igman, an AMX 10 RC of the 1er REC is followed by two Warrior armoured infantry fighting vehicles of 1st Bn., The Devonshire & Dorset Regiment. The deployment of the heavy elements of the RRF on Mount Igman from 23 July 1995 allowed UN troops to stop Serbian attacks on the so-called Log Track – Sarajevo's only supply road, in the direction of Mostar. It also secured observation of the Serbian positions in the whole Sarajevo area, and the direction of air and artillery support. The British and French units got on well together, to the extent that the CO of 1DDR was made an honorary private first class of the 2e REI – a rare compliment.

(Below) Protected inside their VAB, the crew of a 2e REI 120mm mortar await their next fire mission. Note the rounds in the bin at left, with their variously coloured incremental propellant charges; that at far left is a smoke round. The mortar crews were only allowed to fire smoke – to 'intimidate' the Serbs! – before 14 July 1995. This changed with the destruction of two Belgian UN vehicles, which attracted 30 HE rounds in return. The change from passive to active UN operations in Bosnia began with the creation of the RRF by the then commander of UNPROFOR, Lieutenant-General Sir Rupert Smith (who had commanded 1st UK Armoured Division in the Gulf War).

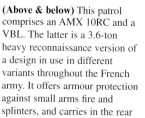

(Above & below) This patrol comprises an AMX 10RC and a VBL. The latter is a 3.6-ton heavy reconnaissance version of a design in use in different variants throughout the French army. It offers armour protection against small arms fire and splinters, and carries in the rear a MILAN firing post and six rounds; an F-1 MG is fixed to a revolving mount over the commander's hatch, and 3,000 rounds are carried. A four-cylinder turbo-diesel gives a top road speed of 95km/h (60mph); it can also be prepared for amphibious operation within two minutes.

(Above) The *képi blanc* is obviously no longer part of the combat uniform of the Legion, but in this kind of operation it still has its uses. It leaves the potential enemy in no doubt about which troops he is facing, and may give him pause before he does anything foolhardy. This gunner mans an F-1 (AA-52) machine gun mounted on the turret of his AMX 10RC.

(Left) The search for hidden weapons caches often led the légionnaires of the IFOR contingent into remote and sometimes heavily mined parts of the country. Here, in March 1996, men of the 3e Escadron, 1er REC observe suspicious movements around one of the many destroyed villages in the neighbourhood of Jablanica. The squadron, together with the 2e REP, was then temporarily under the control of Brigade Champeau of the MNDSE.

45

2e Régiment Étranger de Parachutistes

Although the 2e REP is one of the youngest regiments of the Legion it is also perhaps the best-known, due to the large number of overseas operations to which it has been committed.

The first Legion parachute unit was the Compagnie Parachutiste of the 3e REI, formed on 1 April 1948 with men drawn from the 2e and 3e REI and 13e DBLE in Indochina. Much of the Indochina War was fought against an elusive enemy in the thickly forested hills of central and northern Vietnam. There was thus a great demand for para-troops – the only type of unit which gave the French army any hope of mounting surprise attacks.

In July 1948 a new 1er Bataillon Étranger de Parachutistes (1er BEP) was raised in North Africa, followed by the 2e BEP that October; both were shipped to Indochina as soon as they had completed jump training. Because of the high casualty rate a 3e BEP was raised in North Africa in November 1949 to feed replacements to the battalions in Indochina.

The Legion paras were committed to all major campaigns during the war: they were dropped into desperate situations as an airborne 'fire brigade', took their part in long search-and-destroy missions as crack light infantry, and defended strongpoints against attack by the ever-stronger Viet Minh. The 1er BEP was wiped out in the terrible fighting on Route Coloniale 4 in October 1950, but was reformed. In winter 1951/52 both battalions fought in the Hoa Binh campaign on RC 6. In November 1953 the 1er BEP and CEPML were part of the force which jumped to secure and consolidate the Dien Bien Phu position. General Giap launched his assault on the besieged camp in March 1954; and on 9 April the 2e BEP jumped in to join the garrison. Survivors of the two BEPs were still fighting as a composite unit when Dien Bien Phu fell on 7 May. Both were immediately reformed.

After the return to Algeria in 1955 the 3e BEP was disbanded, and the 1er and 2e were expanded into the 1er and 2e REPs. From 1956 to 1962 these regiments saw constant action and achieved great successes in the war against the

(Top of page) Regimental breast and beret badges of the 2e REP. The former incorporates the Legion grenade and colours with a Chinese dragon, recalling the 2e BEP's battles in Indochina; the latter is worn by all French army airborne units apart from Marine regiments.

(Below) At last he has qualified for his wings, and the CO pins the *brevet de parachutiste* on the chest of a proud young légion-naire. As a full member of the 2e REP he now also receives the lanyard in the ribbon colour of the Légion d'Honneur granted to the 2e BEP in 1954. All members of a unit so honoured wear the *fourragère,* while the medal itself is pinned to the regimental flag. Note these different uniforms: the *caporal* at left wears the old service dress (with the 11e DP patch on the shoulder), the colonel wears the green F-1 combat fatigues, while the new paratrooper has received the latest *blouson* uniform in *terre de France* colour.

Algerian FLN. When it became clear that the French government was going to withdraw from the Legion's Algerian 'homeland' there was a tragic mutiny in April 1961 by several units, including the 1er REP; it failed, and this élite regiment was disbanded.

The 2e REP survived this unhappy period; it was transferred to the Quartier Raffali at Calvi, Corsica, and in June 1967 came under the 11e Division Parachutiste, which remains its higher formation. Under the wise command of Colonel Caillaud the regiment transformed itself from straightforward airmobile infantry into a para-commando unit with many specialist skills. Its first deployment to Chad in 1969 was followed by others in 1978, 1984 and 1987. Companies rotated through Djibouti to operate alongside the 13e DBLE; and in February 1976 men of the 2e REP freed a busload of schoolchildren kidnapped by terrorists on the Djibouti/Somalia border.

On 19 May 1978 Colonel Erulin's 2e REP made its most famous combat jump when it was dropped over Kolwezi in Zaire's Shaba province to rescue some 2,000 European civilians trapped by Congolese rebels.

In 1982 the regiment was sent into war-torn Beirut as part of the multi-national force (Operation Epaulard); in 1990 it served in Rwanda; and in 1991 its élite recce-commando section was in the Gulf for Operation Daguet. Within six months in 1993 the 2e REP found itself in both Somalia and Bosnia with the UN forces. In 1995 the paras were back in Bosnia, followed by a tour in Chad in 1996, and participation

(Above) The 3e Cie. – note black scarves around their left shoulders – specialises in amphibious operations. Here part of the company is training in Zodiacs off the Corsican coast near Calvi, where the regiment maintains its own amphibious training centre.

(Left) Once on the ground lack of vehicles restricts paratroopers' mobility. To provide a minimum of mobility French paratroops have the Lohr Fardier FL 501, of which six can be parachuted on pallets by a C-160 transport. It weighs 680kg (1,500lbs), and can officially carry a 500kg (1,100lb) load; it can also tow a trailer with another 600kg (1,320lbs) or a 120mm mortar. In fact it is often used to transport a whole squad – like these men from 4e Cie. – although you can bet that nine légionnaires and their kit weigh more than the official limit! With a top speed of 80km/h (50mph), the FL 501 has a range of 200km (125 miles).

in Operation Pélican II in Congo-Brazzaville in 1997.

The regiment today has 1,500 all ranks, divided into a Command & Services Company (CCS), Recce & Support Company (CEA), 1st, 2nd, 3rd and 4th Combat Companies, and since 1994 a 5th Equipment & Repair Company. Each combat company has a command group, three rifle platoons, and a fire support platoon with two MILAN and two 81mm mortars. Apart from the jump training, and the high level of infantry skills - in all types of terrain and climate - which are demanded of all 2e REP recruits, each company specialises in certain combat scenarios: 1er Cie., urban fighting and night operations; 2e Cie., mountain and cold weather fighting; 3e Cie., amphibious operations; 4e Cie., sabotage and sniping.

The CEA controls a mortar platoon with six 120mm tubes; a cannon platoon with six 20mm weapons; a recce platoon with eight P4 vehicles; and two anti-tank platoons with a total of eight MILAN and four 12.7mm HMGs, mounted in 14 P4s. The long distance recce platoon is also part of this company, and was formerly known as the Commando de Renseignement et d'Action en Profondeur (giving the unfortunate English acronym CRAP – the humour of which it was lethally dangerous to point out to any member of the team). Today the recce platoons of all the 11e DP para units are assembled for operations into a Groupement de Commandos Parachutistes (GCP). This asset can be employed at different levels to support operations ranging from regimental to divisional. Its tasks include locating and marking drop zones as 'pathfinders', deep penetration reconnaissance, sabotage behind enemy lines, hostage rescue, etc.; its members are highly qualified in many skills, including HALO and HAHO parachute insertion.

The regimental CCS fulfills all adminstrative and command tasks, the latter through one or more Tactical Headquarters (EMT); the 2e REP is flexibly structured so as to be capable of limited independent operations. This flexibility, coupled with high mobility, large size, a generous and varied scale of equipment and high levels of competence in a wide range of combat skills, ensure that the 2e REP will remain one of France's most valuable combat assets - and that the légionnaire who achieves its punishing standards has a better chance than most of seeing action.

The 5e Compagnie provides logistic support. Consisting of a catering company, one maintenance and two transport platoons, it is competent to maintain all the vehicles and equipment which the 2e REP possess or may be assigned for particular operations, from P4 jeeps to VAB armoured personnel carriers and Zodiac inflatable craft, from MILAN to the latest satellite communications apparatus.

(Opposite below) Unlike recruits to other French army parachute units, légionnaires do not undergo jump training at the Airborne Troops' School (ETAP) at Pau, but with the 2e REP at Calvi. The course lasts three to four weeks, and involves intensive theoretical and practical ground training before the first jump. Here trainees wait for a despatcher to check that their main and reserve 'chutes and jump pack container are faultlessly fitted before they emplane.

(Right) During their regimental jump training 2e REP pupils must complete six jumps in the following order: (1) without pack; (2) without pack, the pupil successfully opening his reserve 'chute; (3) with pack; (4 & 5) with pack and weapons; (6) with pack and weapons at night.

Among its many other tasks the regiment's 5e Cie. is responsible for packing 17,000 parachutes, of six different types, each year.

(Below) A Legion para prepares for landing; he has dropped his pack container to hang on its quick-release line below him. French paratroopers are issued the well-proven EPI 'chute; its canopy is smaller than the widely used American T-10, giving a faster descent – this cuts the time he is in the air, at maximum risk from ground fire.
(Photo Carl Schulze)

(Below right) During the Franco-British exercise Winged Crusader 93 on Corsica, paras of the 1er Cie. collect heavy equipment containers on the drop zone – coloured flags help identify assembly points. This phase is the most dangerous of any airborne operation, since the troops are still scattered and no effective defence is yet possible.
(Photo Carl Schulze)

(Left) One of the GCP's tasks is prisoner rescue; here a team armed with MP5-SD3 silenced sub-machine guns and Beretta pistols enter a building for a simulated hostage rescue. They wear special operations overalls with thigh holsters and magazine pockets. Like all such special forces the GCP commandos are trained in careful reconnaissance beforehand, so that they can eliminate the hostage-takers in seconds without additional danger to their captives.

(Right) One of the 4e Cie. specialities is explosives; here charges are connected up with detonation cord. Note the company scarf and helmet marking. After passing jump school the new member of the 2e REP receives integration training in his new company, and specialist training to prepare him for his task within the company. As his years of service pass he will receive continuing up-grading in his specialty, and cross-training in extra skills.

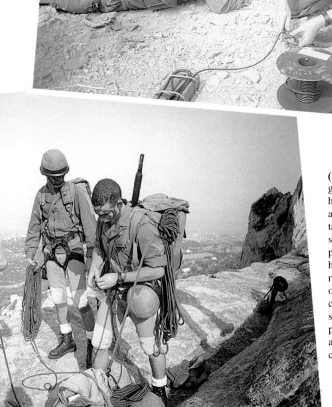

(Left) Corsica is an ideal training ground for para-commandos. It has beaches and steep cliffs for amphibious training, high mountains for climbing and winter snows for skiing. There are level plains for parachute jumps and helicopter training, but also rugged hills and gorges for orienteering exercises and rapid cross-country marches to build stamina. Here men of the 2e Cie. prepare to climb a cliff face above Camp Raffali, carrying combat rucksacks and weapons.

(Right) The 4e Cie. were among the first units of the Rapid Reaction Force to receive the American .50cal Barrett sniper rifle. Its employment by 2e REP counter-sniper teams in Sarajevo provided valuable experience and contributed greatly to the development of a doctrine for its effective use. This sniper wears a typical 'ghillie suit', sewn all over with long strips of rag to help break up his outline and merge with the background.

(Right) The 3e Cie. regularly train in collaboration with submarines and surface vessels of the French navy. Here légion-naire-paras are boarding the submarine which will be their home for several days. They will be infiltrated ashore as frogmen, leaving the submerged boat through a torpedo tube or a special hatch.

(Left) For one week every month a C-160 Transall is made available to the 2e REP for jump training. As well as initial instruction, members of the regiment must make regular duty jumps to keep up their qualification status. The long 'sticks' of paratroopers leave the aircraft at very short intervals, and this must be practised frequently to avoid accidents. Note the triangular assembly markings on the helmets, here those of the 2e and 5e Compagnies.

Operation Turquoise: the Legion in Rwanda

Since the former Belgian colony of Rwanda achieved independence in 1963 this small, fertile central African country has been torn by periodic and ever-bloodier clashes between the two tribes which make up the mass of the population: the Hutus, in the great majority, and the minority Tutsis. The latter, who are of a more Nilotic origin, were traditionally dominant. When the Hutu President Juvénel Habayarimana was killed in an aircraft crash on 6 April 1994, Hutu fanatics turned on the Tutsis – and any moderate Hutus who tried to save them – and instigated a wave of massacres more savage and more widespread than ever before. At a conservative estimate some half a million men, women and children were butchered with great cruelty, often by their former neighbours.

A large number of Tutsis were already living in exile in Uganda since previous outbreaks of violence; with Ugandan assistance they had formed a well-organised armed force, the Front Patriotique Rwandais (FPR). This now crossed the border to save, or at least to avenge their tribespeople. The Rwandan government army (FAR) was already weakened by a UN embargo, and the FPR made rapid progress. In July the towns of Butare, Gitamara and Gisenyi and the capital Kigali fell to the Tutsi army, which then controlled about a third of the country. Huge numbers of both Hutu and surviving Tutsi populations were now displaced after fleeing their homes.

In May 1994 the UN Security Council had authorised the engagement of a 5,000-strong peace-keeping force for the protection of the refugees of the civil war and to oversee a humanitarian aid operation, under the title MINUR II (Mission des Nations Unis au Rwanda). Early in this operation it became clear that the mission objectives would change, due both to the unreadiness of some African contingents promised to the UN force, and to continued military successes by the FPR. In effect, France interpreted the mission as partly to prevent further Tutsi advances.

The UN authorised France – which on 22 June announced its readiness to set up a protection zone before the arrival of MINUR II troops – to intervene in order to save what could be saved. The next day the first 500 men from the French special units standing by at Goma and Buka in neighbouring Zaire arrived at Cyangugu; on the 24th another 1,000 followed, including men of the 2e REI. In the meantime the French air force transferred four Mirage F-1CR and four F-1CT fighters to Kigali for air support, with four Jaguars standing by at Bangui in the Central African Republic.

In all the French Operation Turquoise would involve 2,500 men and 5,000 tons of equipment being transferred to Rwanda. These included the 1er Cie., 2e REI; 3e Cie., 13e DBLE; HQ and CRAP, 2e REP; together with parts of the 2e and 3e RPIMa, 11e RAMa with 120mm mortars, and 2e RICM with 12 AMX 90 light armoured cars.

The HQ of the combat unit of the Legion, which was to control the extreme south-west of Rwanda, was set up at Kamembe airfield, Cyangugu; it was comanded by Colonel Hogard of the 13e Demi-Brigade. In the west and south the Legion sector ran up to the state's borders with Zaire and Burundi; the north and east, where the French sector abutted territory held by the FPR, were the responsibility of the marine paras and artillery.

The Legion prepared to relieve any worsening of the situation of the French marines stationed east of them and to protect Gikongoro from an advance by the FPR; in fact this threat did not materialise. For the légionnaires of the 3e/13e

(Left) Lieutenant of the 1er Cie., 2e REI (note the two gold rank bars) photographed during a patrol along the Ruzizi river. They were searching for armed bands of former Rwandan soldiers and militia; after many hours' march through plantations and thick jungle reminiscent of the old days in Indochina they seized 20 weapons. The officer carries a FAMAS rifle, a more practical weapon in the field than the 9mm pistol, which is only useful for self defence at very short range. His radio is a TR-PP-11B.

(Opposite) Patrols were daily routine for the légionnaires in Rwanda. Here snipers of the 3e Séction, 3e Compagnie, 13e DBLE ride a VLRA light truck along a dirt road east of Lake Kivu. The man in the white shirt is a UN Prefect, getting an escorted overview of the damage caused by the civil war. Note the .50cal Barrett rifles carried by two of the section. The tactical marking on the truck fender identifies company, regiment, and French Forces in Djibouti – the 13e Demi-Brigade's home base.

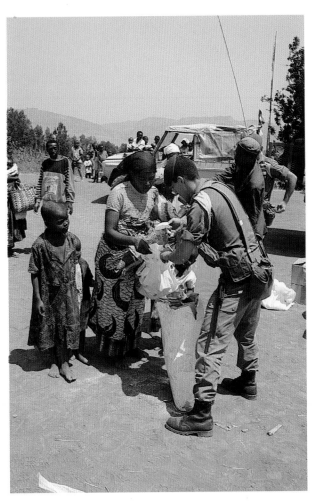

(Left) Humanitarian aid was also a priority once the security zone had been established. Here légionnaires distribute flour to civilians in the square in front of Nyamashe church – where more than 800 Tutsi were massacred only a matter of weeks before. The yellow scarf around the shoulder identifies the 3e Cie. of the 13e DBLE; this system of company colours is customary throughout the French army, although the sequence differs from unit to unit.

(Below left) The semi-automatic Barrett .50cal sniper rifle puts immense firepower at the disposal of the team. Equally, the legend of the Foreign Legion goes before them, and the respect it engendered among potential opponents allowed a process of de-escalation in their sector of Rwanda. For the same reason légionnaires prefer to wear their green berets instead of the standard Spectra helmets whenever possible.

(Opposite) In front of Capitaine Bourchez's P4 vehicle the results of a search operation are displayed. Amongst these are Chinese and American hand grenades, an Uzi sub-machine gun, an FN Hi-Power pistol, and various AK-47 series assault rifles. Note the légionnaire at left foreground; he has a large torch taped under his FAMAS, for use when searching dark African huts, and he has acquired a set of chest webbing – perhaps of African origin.

(Below) Foot patrol by men of the 1er Cie., 2e REI. The légionnaire of today can call on the Legion's extensive experience of operations in Africa stretching back several decades.

DBLE the operation began with a race against time; directly after arriving they had to drive the 100km (62 miles) to Kitabi, to take up positions on the only passage through the Nyungwe Forest in case of an FPR advance – which did not occur.

During the next three weeks the légionnaires and marines succeeded in gaining control over the security zone so that humanitarian organisations could take up their task – this was achieved despite the FPR capture of Butare and Kigali, and a minor clash between FPR troops and French special forces at the former town on 3 July. A larger encounter occurred on 14 July, and over the next fortnight clashes – often involving mortar fire by both sides – took place at several points on the border of the security zone. A truce was concluded at the end of the month, which simplified the situation for the légionnaires.

From then on it was a question of supervising the refugee camps, distributing humanitarian aid, and ensuring security and order on the streets of Rwandan towns. On 5 August the first MINUR II troops arrived and were integrated into Operation Turquoise. Many Hutus distrusted them, since they remembered the failure of MINUR I, and believed that the UN troops were biased in favour of the Tutsis. They also resented African contingents which spoke English – the language of the FPR's Ugandan allies – and only Senegalese, Congolese and Guinean troops succeeded in gaining their trust. The MINUR force was later strengthened by troops from Britain, Canada, Australia, Ghana and Ethiopia, and led by the Canadian General Tousignant.

The last French troops left Rwanda on 22 August 1994. As well as establishing peace and order in the security zones they had flown in and distributed 10,980 tons of humanitarian aid. French medical teams of the Élement Médical d' Intervention Rapide (EMIR), under the protection of the Legion, had carried out 691 emergency operations, treated 91,300 patients and rendered first aid to 75,000 more. At the same time, to prevent epidemics, some 30,000 bodies had been buried in mass graves.

In July 1994 the Nyarushishi camp sheltered some 12,000 refugees – overwhelmingly Tutsis. As can be seen, the shelter provided was of the most primitive sort, but it gave better protection than hiding in the bush – where the refugees also faced the risk of being slaughtered. The légionnaires guarded the camp round the clock and ensured peace and order within it; this man's blue shoulder scarf identifies him as from 1er Cie., 2e REI.

(Left) The region around the Nyumgwe Forest is known as 'the Land of a Thousand Hills'. Here pairs of légionnaires of the 3e/13e hold widely dispersed positions allowing surveillance from above of the woodland within the tea plantation which stretches away to the east.

(Opposite top) A 13e DBLE rifle squad sniper armed with an FR-F2 keeps observation on movement in a tea plantation from a bunker on the edge of the Nyungwe Forest; these positions were made strong enough to give overhead protection from mortar fire. Note the grenades lying close to hand: a DF-37 fragmentation and an OF-37 blast grenade. These antiques still work, but they are relics of the 1930s, when many armies provided different types of equipment for different antici-pated battle scenarios.

(Below) The légionnaires carried out frequent vehicle checks at points along the main road of the French security zone; these often led to the seizure of weapons and arrest of suspects. It is worth drawing attention to the transistor radio carried by one man in the back of the pink truck. In Rwanda massacres were often triggered by calls to murder the people of the other tribe, broadcast by transmitters operated by various factions. There was a naive belief that anything broadcast over the radio must be true.

(Opposite below) Colonel Hogard's légionnaires set up a local police troop, armed with weapons taken from Hutu FAR soldiers fleeing to the Zaire border – like these men, handing over their FAL rifles to a member of the 2e REP Deep Recce & Action Commando. This crack unit controlled and supervised the police, who were distinguished by yellow berets. The Legion para-commandos also carried out operations against bands of looters and killers who had taken refuge on the islands in Lake Kivu.

59

3e Régiment Étranger d'Infanterie

In 1915, after the several 'marching regiments' drawn from the 1er and 2e RE for service on the Western Front had suffered heavy casualties, the Legion troops in France were gathered into a single three-battalion Régiment de Marche de la Légion Étrangère (RMLE). Commanded from 1917 by Colonel Rollet, the RMLE covered itself with glory, ending the war with its status as one of the two most highly decorated regiments in the entire French army marked by a double lanyard. In January 1921, as part of the post-war reorganisation of the Legion, the RMLE was retitled the 3rd Foreign Infantry. It returned to Morocco, where during the interwar years it both fought in many campaigns and made a large

contribution to building up the infrastructure of the country.

After the Allied landings in French North Africa in late 1942 the 3e REI fought against the German Afrika Korps in Tunisia in spring 1943, acquitting itself well despite its out-of-date equipment, but suffering heavy casualties. It was disbanded, and its surviving members (and traditions) were transferred to the newly formed 'second' RMLE. This unit provided the mechanised infantry for the new French 5th Armoured Division, which landed in southern France in 1944 and had fought its way into Austria by VE-Day. Retitled the 3e REI in 1945, the regiment served with distinction in Indochina (including famous battles such as Phu Tong Hoa, Dong Khe, RC 4 and Dien Bien Phu) and in Algeria.

After Algerian independence the 3e REI was stationed from 1962 to 1973 in Madagascar, where it came to specialise in both amphibious and jungle operations, developing the basis for what has since become the French army's tropical warfare training programme. In 1973 the regiment transferred to French Guiana (Guyane) on the South

(Top of page) Regimental breast and beret badges of the 3e REI; the former was originally that of the RMLE during World War II.
(Below) A 'snowcat' in the tropics. The Hägglund BV 206 is an articulated amphibious vehicle whose four broad rubber tracks deliver a very low ground pressure, making it suitable for swampy terrain. It weighs 4.5 tons and has a load capacity of 2.5 tons. Six légionnaires can be accomodated in the front cab; the rear cab has various formats, but here it too is fitted for troop transport. The Mercedes six-cylinder diesel engine gives a top speed of 52km/h (32mph) on land and 3km/h (1.8mph) in water.

American coast, where it is still stationed at Quartier Forget, Kourou. The regiment comes under the control of the Forces Armées aux Antilles-Guyane (FAAG). Its special responsibilities include the Centre Spatial Guyanais (CSG) – the core of the European space programme, ideally sited on the equator at Kourou; and the Centre d'Entrainement en Fôret Équatoriale (CEFE) – the French army's jungle warfare school.

The regiment, 880 strong, is divided between the Command & Services Company (CCS), the Recce & Support Company (CEA) and two Combat Compagnies. A unique feature is that during the periodic launches of Ariane rockets from the nearby CSG it is reinforced by an extra rifle company from France, which may be from a Legion or a conventional French unit.

Responsible for all command, administration and logistics, the CCS has signals, medical, transport and maintenance platoons. Besides the usual land transport it has at its disposal Swedish BV 206 tracked vehicles; a maritime section with CTM landing craft for coastal operations; and two Tanguy craft for operations on inland waterways. The CCS also provides the personnel for three out-stations in the jungle.

The CEA comprises a reconnaissance platoon, a pioneer platoon, an anti-aircraft platoon with 20mm cannons and MISTRAL rocket systems; and, uniquely, two 'ultralight' aircraft, ideally suited for local reconnaissance. The two Combat Companies share the other tasks of the regiment. Currently the 2e Cie. is responsible for the protection of Kourou and the regional transport centre, while the 3e Cie. carries out patrols in the jungle and on the Oyapock river along the Surinam and Brazilian borders.

The CEFE jungle training centre at Camp Szuts provides 26 three-week courses for 1,500 French and foreign students each year (each member of the 3e REI must also pass the course at least once during his two-year posting). Run by instructors with several years' jungle experience, the CEFE course teaches all the essential skills of survival – navigation and movement, finding food, making fire, protection against hazards and illnesses – as well as the use of small arms in the tropical environment, and the exploitation of minimal personal equipment during prolonged jungle operations.

Apart from its special missions, the 3e REI is responsible for supporting French interests throughout the region. It can mobilise an efficient operational unit of 500 all ranks, for transfer at short notice by sea or air. This unit is designated Détachement Jaguar.

(Above right) For protection of the European space centre at Kourou from air attack the 3e REI is equipped with the Matra MISTRAL. This infra-red guided system has a lateral range of 6km (3.72 miles) and a ceiling of 4.5km (14,763ft); the HE head has both impact and proximity fuzes. With a total weight of 40kg (88lbs) the launch post and rocket can be broken down into five main components in three man-loads.

(Right) During launch programmes for the Ariane rocket at Kourou the 3e REI carry out round-the-clock patrols.

(Left & below) Tanguy craft are used for patrols on the Oyapock river in the Brazilian and Surinam border areas; smuggling gangs carry on a brisk trade between the three countries. These men of the 2e Cie., their cap badges covered against reflection, carry FAMAS rifles and Mossberg shotguns.

(Above) MISTRAL gunner in training.

(Opposite top) Even in the tropics the traditional uniform and accoutrements of the Legion are worn for guard order. This *caporal* on sentry duty at Quartier Forget in Kourou wears summer khaki shirtsleeve uniform with the white képi, green and red epaulettes and blue waist sash. Above the two green rank chevrons on his right sleeve the shoulder patch of the FAAG can just be seen under the epaulette fringe. His right breast insignia include the US Presidential Citation ribbon earned by the RMLE in World War II. Obscured here by his FAMAS is the 3e REI's massive triple lanyard in the colours of the Légion d'Honneur, Médaille Militaire and Croix de Guerre 1914-18, marking the regiment's unique record of 16 citations in army orders – see page 3.

(Opposite below) Légionnaires make one of their regular checks on a service road at the Kourou space centre. They also carry out frequent patrols along the few roads through the jungles of Guyane, not only to watch for smugglers and to provide general security but also to check surface conditions – in the rainy season the roads are often washed out. In such cases the 3e REI pioneer platoon is called out to make repairs.

(Left & below) Maintaining physical fitness is one of the fundamentals of survival in the jungle. This is repeatedly tested during the first two weeks of the three-week CEFE course at Camp Szuts. At the same time students are prepared for the final exercise, a week-long jungle patrol. Intensive training in temperatures of 40°C (105°F) and 90% humidity demands a regular intake of water, and each man is responsible for providing for himself.

(Above) An impeccably turned-out sentry stands by a memorial in the form of a statue of a légionnaire equipped for the tropical expeditions of the late 19th century, recalling the Legion's many dead – mostly from disease – in Dahomey, Madagascar and Tonkin.

(Above) The staff at the CEFE instruct the students in all the hazards of living and travelling in the jungle. In fact, however, the greatest dangers come not from constricting snakes like this king python, or from jaguars, but from insignificant or invisible foes – insects, blood-sucking parasites, and the diseases lurking in bad drinking water. If disregarded the smallest scratch can quickly lead to inflammation and infection in the humid climate, and the chafing of clothes and equipment on constantly wet skin causes painful skin disorders. Even if an injury is not dangerous in itself, the injured man represents an additional burden for the group.

(Above right) Légionnaire of the 2e Cie. (red scarf) prepares for a jungle patrol of several days' duration. The men are dropped off by boat or helicopter; from then on they must rely on their own resources. The exhausting routine of marching through thick jungle is only broken by the occasional visit to one of the remote Indian villages.

(Right) During both routine jungle operations and the CEFE course the légionnaire lives off the country – and the menu can be extensive, if you know what is edible and where to find it. The spectrum ranges from tropical fruit through roots, mammals, fish, birds and reptiles to insects.

Détachement de Légion Étrangère de Mayotte

When in 1975 the Comoro Islands were granted independence, the population of the south-eastern island of Mayotte voted in a referendum to remain under French governance; and this secession took place the following April. This tiny volcanic island, the last remnant of France's Indian Ocean colonies, is of strategic importance. It lies in the Mozambique Channel, which in the event of a blockade of the Suez Canal would be one of the main shipping routes between the Middle East oilfields and Europe.

Since November 1967 a detachment from the 3e REI, then in Madagascar, had been stationed on Mayotte; but it was only in April 1973 that the unit was designated Foreign Legion Comoro Detachment (DLEC), and, after the island's secession, DLEM. In 1984 the DLEM took over the standard and traditions of the former 2e Régiment Étranger de Cavalerie, which had been disbanded on 31 July 1962 after the Algerian War. The unit is controlled by the Forces Armées dans la Zone de l'Océan Indien (FAZOI).

The DLEM has a 110-strong Command & Supply Squadron (ECS) stationed permanently on Mayotte, together with a rifle company – Legion or otherwise – from the Force d'Action Rapide on a four-month rotation. The main barracks is at Daudzi in the east, with a detachment at Kwale in the south. The DLEM carries out numerous exercises with French naval and air force units in the Indian Ocean. It is tasked with demonstrating a French presence in the region, with the support of civilian and military authorities in the maintenance of security and order, and with maintaining readiness as a regional intervention force. In times of crisis it can deploy to strategically important points in its region and prepare for the reception of larger forces, e.g. the FAR.

In 1989 French troops were deployed in Operation Oside to restore democracy in the troubled Comoro Islands. In 1995 Mayotte again provided the jumping-off point for intervention there when French troops put down the mercenary rebellion led by Bob Denard; this Operation Azalée took just half a day.

(Top of page) The breast badge of the DLEM. Although the detachment guards the standard and traditions of the disbanded 2e REC they do not wear cavalry silver uniform lace and buttons.

(**Left**) Exercises with units of the other French armed services stationed in or deployed to the Indian Ocean region are frequent. These légionnaires of the DLEM assemble after being flown in by a French air force Transall.

Two Transalls lifted the DLEM rifle company to Hahaya airfield in the Comoros in 1995, securing it in half an hour against the mercenary rebellion led by Bob Denard. Marines then flew in to quash the rising. (Photo *Képi Blanc*)

(**Below**) A *caporal-chef* of the DLEM instructs Madagascan soldiers on the operation of an 81mm mortar during a training exercise in Madagascar. Relations between that country and France have improved in recent years, and such exercises are becoming more common. (Photo *Képi Blanc*)

(**Opposite**) Changing the guard at the garrison at Dzaoudzi, the home of the Legion detachment on Mayotte. The commander of the DLEM is also in control of the personnel of all three French armed services on the island – note his rank of lieutenant-colonel. The Legion maintains and guards the island's fuel supply. (Photo *Képi Blanc*)

Operation Almandine II: the Legion in the Central African Republic

The Central African Republic is a small, arid, flyblown ex-French colony strategically located at the heart of the north/central region of the continent, and blessed with certain mineral deposits. It has often been the site for Legion operations; and France has maintained two bases there, at Bangui and Bouar, as jumping-off points for intervention throughout the area. The CAF also offers ideal conditions for training in bush warfare.

In 1979 légionnaires and other French troops presided over the almost bloodless removal of the increasingly eccentric dictator 'Emperor' Bokassa in Operation Barracuda; formerly a loyal ally whose excesses were overlooked, he had overtaxed French patience when human body parts were found in his refrigerator. The previously docile former colony went through some more volatile periods thereafter; and in 1996-97 Legion paratroopers took part in quelling an insur-

rection by parts of the Central African Republic's army (Forces Armées Centrafricaines, FACA).

In November 1996 the FACA were disturbed by their third mutiny since April. The rebels' aim was – once more – to secure the payment of long-overdue army wages, but also to depose President Ange Patassé. The majority of the rebel troops came from the Yakoma tribe – the 'People of the River' – who represented only about 5% of the population. However, Yakomas made up about 40% of the FACA, since the previous president was from this tribe and had favoured it when recruiting for the forces. The mutineers found support in some suburbs of Bangui, and there was heavy fighting for control of the radio stations.

French troops intervened to obtain a truce, enforcing the status quo so that negotiations could take place. The French occupied positions between the camps of the mutineers and the president's guard; the rebels, led by Captain Anicet Saulet, had control of the FACA's heavy weapons. Tension grew throughout December 1996, and France sent reinforcements from Chad, in particular the 3e and 4 Cies. and Deep Recce & Action Commando of the 2e REP. During civil unrest among Yakomas in the Kouanga quarter of Bangui a

(Below) From the roof of a telecommunications building in western Bangui paras of the 2e REP keep watch over the suburb of Petevo. Photographed during a period of high tension, they wear Spectra helmets and body armour. The covers for the helmet and splinter-proof vest are in the new *tenue camouflée*, already introduced for the complete uniform to units in Bosnia; the fatigues here are still the old olive green *treillis F-1* worn by the Legion since the 1960s.

(Right) This légionnaire of the 2e REP is armed with the new 5.56mm Minimi light machine gun which during the 1990s took over from the old 7.5mm AA-52 (NAAT F-1) as the infantry squad's integral light automatic support weapon. The gas-operated Minimi weighs 7.1kg (15.5lbs) – about 7lbs lighter than the AA-52 – and fires the same ammunition as the standard FAMAS rifle, in either 200-round belts held in this box carrier, or 30-round magazines; it thus offers the légionnaire considerable practical advantages over its predecessor. It has a combat range of up to 1,000m, and a theoretical rate of fire of 700 to 1,000rpm. The AA-52 is still used in vehicle mountings.

(Below) Despite the problems in the town of Bangui regular training was carried on. This Legion NCO from Alsace, working with a red-beret marine para of 8e RPIMa, prepares to mark a landing zone for a parachute exercise on the airfield at Bangui. Jumping here is an adventure with a flavour all its own: as he lands the paratrooper often finds himself confronting a crowd of 'godobeds' – young Africans who live by theft, and who are ambitious enough to try to steal a parachute. Their attentions in the streets of Bangui are a plague to the local population, who show no mercy if they catch one.

French captain and an NCO were shot dead by a mutineer. The French government decided to intervene, and Operation Almandine II was planned for the night of 4/5 January 1997. The aim of the operation was to gain control of the suburbs of Bakongo and Kouanga and to put pressure on the rebel HQ in Camp du Kasai.

General Coste set up his command post in Camp Beal; his troops were divided between Tactical HQs (EMTs) South and North. EMT Sud under Colonel Leclerc had its command post in the president's palace; it comprised the 2e and 4e Cies., 3e RIMa; 1er Cie., 2e RIMa; and from 5 January, the marine paras of the 1er Cie., 8e RPIMa, flown in from Gabon. EMT Nord was commanded by Colonel Puga, CO of the 2e REP, and comprised the Deep Recce & Action Commando, 3e and 4e Cies. of his regiment plus the 2e Cie., 8e RPIMa. For fire support each EMT also had at its disposal one platoon of AML 90 armoured cars from the 1er Esc., 1er RIMa, and one of VLRA trucks mounting 20mm cannon of the 11e RAMa. Two Puma helicopters, the rest of the 1er/1er RIMa, and a 120mm mortar platoon from the 11e RAMa were available in reserve.

On the night of 4/5 January it in fact fell to the 2e/8e RPIMa to take Kouanga, and the 2e REP seized control of Bakongo; the support of the Pumas, with 20mm GIAT electrically operated cannon mounted as door guns, also contributed to this success. Small incidents followed on the night of the 10th, when a soldier of the 4e/2e REP killed an armed civilian who was threatening the local population; and on the night of the 16th, when there was a brief exchange of fire between mutineers and a patrol from the 3e/2e REP – one rebel was killed and the rest retreated under mortar fire.

In February the French reinforcements left the country, being relieved by African peace-keepers of the Inter-African Mission for Surveillance of the Bangui Accords (MISAB). France intends to give up her two bases in the CAF; indeed, officially all French troops have already left in order to take up their future garrison at N'djamena in Chad.

(Left) A member of the 2e REP's Deep Recce & Action Commando patrolling a Yakoma area of the capital. All seems peaceful – and after months of unrest and economic disruption most of the local population certainly welcomed the stability restored by the French. Even so, in Africa any crowd can turn into a violent mob at short notice; foreign troops, in particular, must remain keenly sensitive to the mood of the moment so as not to provoke a dangerous situation. Note that this commando is armed with a 9mm pistol in a thigh holster as well as his rifle.

(Below) A patrol of légionnaires from the 4e Cie., 2e REP pass through Kouanga, which a few days before had been one of the rebel strongholds. The tension has relaxed; the troops wear their berets instead of helmets, and have left behind their body armour. All the same, many such patrols did carry the squad's LRAC 89mm anti-tank rocket launcher as well as their FAMAS rifles; the mutineers had taken possession of the FACA's heavy weapons.

(Right) Traffic on the approach roads to Bangui was controlled during the crisis by joint 2e REP/FACA checkpoints. Vehicles loaded to the limit of their capacity, in the typical local fashion, made ideal hiding places for illegal arms and explosives.

(Left) Puma helicopter in Armée de Terre camouflage and markings, one of two operated in Bangui during Operation Almandine II by the Commandement des Operations Speciales (COS). Apart from their 20mm cannon, the crews' night vision equipment was particularly useful during the take-over of Kouanga and Bakongo by the marine and Legion paras (the mutineers' Camp du Kasai was also taken under fire). The opposition, who lacked such equipment, often gave away their positions while firing on the helicopters.

(Below) Detail of the GIAT 20mm cannon mount in the side door of the COS Puma.

13e Demi-Brigade de Légion Étrangère

Raised in February 1940 at Sidi-bel-Abbès, the 13e DBLE was intended as part of an intervention force to fight with the Finns against the Soviet invasion, but Finland fell too soon. The new unit, equipped and trained for winter warfare, was then committed to help resist the German invasion of Norway. They distinguished themselves at Narvik, but on returning to France found the German *blitzkrieg* already almost victorious. The 13e sailed for England; and for the next two years they were a mainstay of De Gaulle's small Free French forces, fighting alongside the British in East and North Africa, and covering themselves with glory at Bir Hakeim and Alamein. They later fought in Tunisia, Italy, and the Vosges.

Shipped to Indochina in December 1945, the 13e served first in the Mekong Delta and later in North Vietnam, where their many battles included Hoa Binh, Na San and Dien Bien Phu. From 1955 to 1962 they served as intervention troops in the Algerian War. In October 1962 the unit was transferred to French Somalia, a strategic position in the 'horn' of East Africa opposite Aden. When this colony became the Republic of Djibouti and concluded a bilateral defence agreement with Paris, the 13e stayed on as part of the permanent Forces Françaises de Djibouti (FFDJ), which also include the 5e RIAOM and other elements of the three armed services.

Today the 13e DBLE has about 700 all ranks, and is the Legion's only mixed-arms unit. Since the disbandment of the 1er and 4e Compagnies it consists of a Command & Services Company (CCS); an engineer Support & Works Company (CAT); a single mechanised infantry company, the 3e Cie. de Combat; and an integral armoured Reconnaissance Squadron (ER). The unit also controls an attached rotating company from the 2e REP; and runs the Centre d'Entrainement Commando (CEC) at Arta Beach. Apart from the Escadron de Reconnaissance, which is located at Queah, the regiment is based at the Quartier Monclar in Djibouti city.

As well as command, administrative and logistic elements

(Opposite, top of page) Breast and beret badges of the 13e DBLE. The Cross of Lorraine proudly commemorates the fact that in 1940-42 the regiment was the only Legion unit fighting with General de Gaulle's Free French Forces. The unique retention of the anachronistic style of unit title is another salute to the World War II regiment.

(Opposite) Introduction of the American .50cal (12.7mm) Barrett M82A1 heavy sniper rifle gave the légionnaires of the 3e/13e a weapon effective out to 1,800m (about a mile) – even against light armoured targets such as APCs. This semi-automatic weapon weighs 12.9kg (27lbs), and takes a ten-round magazine. The snipers train intensively alongside the MILAN crews of the CCS, learning to counter enemy armour most effectively.

(Above) The green beret was first worn by the Legion paratroopers in Indochina, though without official authority. It was adopted by all Legion units by c.1960, and ever since then has been as much the symbol of the légionnaire in the field as is the white képi on parade.

(Above right) A 120mm mortar crew of the CCS occupies a position excavated by the CAT engineers. An experienced crew can send between 15 and 18 bombs a minute out to targets as much as 13km (8 miles) away, giving French infantry units a uniquely heavy integral fire support asset. Legion crews are trained to take no more than ten minutes to arrive at a position, carry out a fire mission, and change to a subsequent position.

(Right) The other main unit of the FFDJ is another mixed-arms regiment, the 5e Régiment Interarmes d'Outre-Mer. They often train together; here men of the 13e DBLE secure a MISTRAL anti-aircraft position of the 2e/5e RIAOM.

the CCS has an anti-tank platoon with six MILAN posts, and a heavy mortar platoon with six 120mm wheeled weapons.

The Recce Squadron has 12 x ECR 90 Sagaie 6x6 armoured cars; armed with a 90mm tank gun, this can be air-lifted in a C-160 Transall together with a VBL. One troop is equipped with VLRA patrol trucks, and there are integral repair and supply elements; the squadron is thus to some extent self-sufficient for operations, and can be transferred at short notice to any crisis point in much of Africa or the Middle East. Most of its personnel are former members of the 1er REC.

(Above) The backbone of the 13e's Recce Squadron is the air-portable ERC 90 Sagaie 6x6 armoured car, with a crew of commander, gunner and driver. The 8.3 ton Sagaie has a range of 700km (435 miles) and a top speed of 95km/h (60mph). It carries 20 rounds for the 90mm F-4 tank gun, and 2,000 rounds for the co-axial and turret-mounted 7.62mm machine guns.

(Right) Légionnaires of the 2e Cie. d'Appui et de Travaux clearing mines for UN troops in Somalia during Opertion Iskoutir. This is a task they may have to perform at any time, so it is frequently practised in the Djibouti desert. When a mine has been located with a probe it is partly uncovered, with great care, and checked to see if it is fitted with a booby-trap to prevent it being lifted safely. The operation is closely supervised here by a sergeant, who will intervene to correct the slightest mistake. The légionnaires' lives depend on their training.

The 2e Cie. d'Appui et de Travaux (CAT) has at its disposal a range of engineering and mine-clearing equipment. The 3e Cie. de Combat consists of three platoons mounted in VAB armoured carriers and VLRA patrol trucks. Each platoon has a different specialist function: reconnaissance, demolitions, and sniping. Its heavy weapons element includes the VAB Tuccan variant, with a 20mm cannon turret, and 81mm mortars.

In spite of the fact that soldiering under a 40°C (105°F) sun in the searing stone deserts makes great demands on the individual, légionnaires enjoy a tour in Djibouti. Its old-time colonial atmosphere has a charm of its own, for those with a romantic regard for tales of 'La Légion du Papa'.

Given Africa's endemic political instability, with frequent civil wars and *coups d'état* in which French interests and lives may be threatened, the 13e DBLE has taken part in numerous operations during the 1990s. In 1991, during the final phase of the wars in Ethiopia and Eritrea, légionnaires of the 13e helped the Djibouti forces to secure their national borders. During this Operation Godoria, 500 men of the regiment checked 30,000 refugees crossing the frontier – mostly members of the Ethiopian government forces fleeing with their families. The Legion confiscated 8,500 small arms, 50 heavy weapons (14.5mm MGs, anti-tank weapons and mortars), and 26 armoured vehicles (BTR-60, ZSU-23-4, T-55 and T-62 tanks). The légionnaires also distributed 200 cubic meters of water and ten tons of provisions.

In 1992 Operation Iskoutir saw légionnaires in northern Somalia, bringing humanitarian aid to a population devastated by three years of civil war. In 1993 elements of the 13e DBLE took part in the UN aid operation UNOSOM II in Somalia (French designation, Operation Oryx). Diapason I and Diapason II in 1994 took men of the 13e to the Yemen to help protect and evacuate Western civilians caught up in a civil war. We have already seen that the 3e/13e took part in Operation Turquoise in Rwanda that same year.

(Above) The Commando Training Centre run by the 13e DBLE is at Camp Sergent Cavanna at Arta Beach on the south coast of the Gulf of Tadjoura. Both French and Djiboutian soldiers are trained here by Legion instructors.

(Right) Engineer vehicles have many uses. Here one of the CAT's Moyens Polyvalents du Génie (MPG – multi-purpose engineer machine) clears a barricade of burning tyres. One of the main operational tasks for the unit engineers in case of crisis is the excavation of concealment positions for the Recce Squadron's ECR 90s in the utterly flat desert on the south-eastern border. It is excellent 'tank country' – but the terrain, the glare and the heat haze make anything that sticks up more than 1.5m (4.9ft) above ground level look about twice as big as it is.

6e Régiment Étranger du Génie

The 6th Foreign Engineer Regiment (6e REG), raised on 1 July 1984, is therefore the youngest operational unit in the Legion; but since it has taken over the number and lineage of a disbanded regiment it can nevertheless look back to an older tradition.

After World War I the former Turkish territory in the Levant – what is now Lebanon and Syria – was granted to France as a mandate territory. Légionnaires of the 4e REI and the 1er REC saw hard fighting there in 1925 during a rising by Druze tribesmen. The 6e Régiment Étranger d'Infanterie was formed in October 1939 from battalions of the 1er and 2e REI which were then in garrison there. In summer 1941, during the Vichy period, a British Commonwealth/Free French force – including the 13e DBLE – successfully invaded Syria. The two Legion regiments clashed in a tragic fratricidal battle. When an armistice was agreed, the officers and men of the 6e REI were given an honourable choice between joining the 13e or being repatriated to France; about 1,000 rallied to De Gaulle. Returned to North Africa, the rump of the 6e was disbanded in January 1942. The regiment was reformed in 1949 in Tunisia, where it carried out internal security duties; but its main role was as a transit unit for drafts to the battalions fighting in Indochina. The 'Régiment de Levant' was disbanded again in 1955.

Throughout the Legion's 170-year history, in peace and war alike, all its units have frequently carried out major 'pioneer tasks' all over the world, from South-East Asia to North Africa and South America. From the early 19th century until the eve of World War II the légionnaire typically spent as much time carrying a pick and shovel as a rifle; he was used, above all, to drive roads through the wilderness, but also to drain swamps, build forts, and to carry out many other types of colonial public works.

(Top of page) Breast and beret badges of the 6e REG. The former is a modification of the old 6e REI emblem, incorporating the Legion's grenade, the ruins of Baalbek in Syria, and the siege cuirass which is the traditional badge of French army engineers.

(Below) For a river insertion DINOPS divers are brought close to enemy lines by rubber boat; they will then proceed alone, carrying weapons, prepared charges and tools for the mission. This may involve up to three hours in the water, finding their way to the target – often in pitch darkness – by map, compass, and judgement of the speed and depth of the water.

In 1939 the 1er REI raised a whole pioneer battalion. During the Indochina War the French were short of all kinds of specialist soldiers, and they gratefully drew on the huge and varied pool of technical skills which the Legion represented to set up many and various specialist companies. In 1971 the 61st Mixed Legion/Engineer Battalion was raised in southern France; but the 6e REG is the first complete Legion engineer regiment (soon to be joined by the new 2e REG, whose formation was announced in 1997).

The 6e REG is based at the Quartier General Rollet at Laudun, France, under the 6th Light Armoured Division. It is divided into a Compagnie de Commandement et de Logistique (CCL), a Compagnie d'Appui (CA), and four Compagnies de Combat. Equipped with the engineer version of the VAB and with MPG multi-purpose engineer vehicles, the companies are responsible for all the normal combat engineer tasks – laying and clearing of mines, construction and destruction of field fortifications, etc. – but are also

(Left & below) Searching out and clearing mines is a central task for the 6e REG, who have already suffered a number of fatalities. The unit's légionnaires have often served tours in various former theatres of war – Kuwait, Bosnia, Somalia, Djibouti and Cambodia, among others – helping to clear the deadly legacy of ordnance which remains scattered or hidden, taking a continued toll of civilian lives. This team wear special armoured vests and thigh protectors of ballistic material; the man with the probe also has a British Mk 6 ballistic helmet with facial protection.

trained to support and carry out different specialist operations. The 1er Cie. specialises in amphibious operations, the 2e in mountain and cold weather operations, the 3e in airborne operations and the 4e in urban operations, with an emphasis on locating and neutralising enemy ordnance. The heavy mechanical equipment is held by the Compagnie d'Appui – excavators, dump-trucks, cranes, low-loaders, bucket-wheel loaders, bulldozers, mine-laying trailers, mine clearing equipment, etc. – and these are issued to the combat companies at need.

As well as the command, administrative and logistic elements, the CCS includes the Spécialistes d'Aide au Franchissement (SAF), experts in the safe supervision of water-crossings; and the Détachement d'Intervention Nautique Operationnel (DINOPS) – combat divers. The DINOPS mission includes the reconnaissance of landing zones and bridgeheads, sabotage raids behind enemy lines, underwater mine clearance, and – at all times – acting as rescue divers in case of accidents during exercises and operations.

Since its formation the 6e REG has provided troops for many operations. In 1989 légionnaires trained Afghan *mujahedeen* in Pakistan to de-activate Russian mines (Operation Salaam). In 1993-95 the 6e supported BATINF 2 & 4 in Sarajevo, and the 2e Cie. took part in Operation Hermine. In 1996 the whole regiment was posted to Rajlovac, Bosnia, to serve as BATGEN for the Multi-National Division South-East of SFOR.

A defence ministry decision of 11 September 1997 gave birth to a new engineer regiment, the 2e Régiment Étranger du Génie; with an establishment of 650 men in three mechanised engineer companies, a support company, a command and services company and a training company, this will be stationed on the Plateau d'Albion under control of the Brigade de Montagne, successor to the former 27e Division d'Infanterie de Montagne. One engineer company has already been formed as part of the 4e RE.

(Above & right) One of the tasks of the regiment's four combat companies is to support units of the 6e Division Légère Blindée in clearing blockades and obstacles and eliminating enemy bunkers. After the engineers have blown up a barricade under covering fire from their comrades, the légionnaires clear resistance from a building with the support of a sapper equipped with a flame-thrower – a fearsome weapon which has a great psychological effect on any enemy.

(Left) During an exercise by units of the Rapid Reaction Force a bulldozer of the 6e REG disembarks from a landing craft. Attached to the back of the vehicle is a large roll of wire mesh, which is spooled out to make a firm trackway up the beach for the wheeled transport which will follow.

(Right) Men of the 3e Cie., 6e REG use one of the regiment's Multi-Purpose Engineer vehicles (MPGs) to clear a 'street barricade' of burning cars during an urban warfare exercise.

(Left) The 6e REG's combat engineer sections have the VAB-Génie variant of the standard armoured personnel carrier. It accomodates nine men and a variety of engineer tools inside, and a rubber dinghy can be stowed on the roof. These légionnaires wait by their vehicle for their platoon's MPG to clear the burning street barricade.

79

(Left) Equipped with this device, towed behind a truck or other vehicle, an experienced crew can lay up to 1,000 HPD anti-tank mines in an hour. The mines are inserted into the slide by hand; as they slip down they are automatically armed, and the trailer releases them in the open at regular intervals.

(Below) A DINOPS combat diver preparing a bridge for blowing. Although he carries a FAMAS for self defence his aim is normally to avoid contact with the enemy – reaching the target unseen under cover of darkness, carrying out the mission, and disappearing unseen before the explosion. DINOPS often carry out joint training with American SEALs and Marine Recon units as well as Spanish and Italian combat divers.

(Left) It was due to the enthusiasm and dedication of regimental officers and men that the DINOPS team was created at unit level, growing from an original small team of safety divers into a powerful and extremely versatile combat asset which draws on the wide range of specialist skills to be found within the ranks of the 6e REG. The légionnaire-frogmen have the most up-to-date equipment and are multi-skilled; they may be inserted using oxygen rebreather equipment – which leaves no tell-tale bubbles on the surface – by rubber boats or kayaks, helicopters or parachute drops. In Iraq in February 1991 they carried out normal combat engineer tasks, helping clear the route of advance for elements of the US 82nd Airborne Division. Shortly afterwards they found themselves back in their special element, clearing mines underwater in Kuwait City's harbour alongside Australian mine-divers.

(Above) For coastal, river or lake insertions the DINOPS teams sometimes use the kayak, photographed here during daytime training. Actual operations are always carried out under cover of darkness, using night vision equipment.

(Left) The DINOPS arsenal includes silenced weapons like the Heckler & Koch MP5-SD3, and more unconventional items such as this crossbow, both of which can be useful for quiet disposal of sentries during sabotage operations.

Operation Pelican II: the Legion in the Congo

In 1997 President Mobutu Sese Sekko, the long-time dictator and looter of Zaire (the former Belgian Congo, now renamed yet again as the Democratic Republic of Congo) was finally forced to flee the country by ill-health and the breakdown of his ramshackle regime. Pelican I was an international operation launched in April 1997 in case of a need to evacuate Western civilians from the capital, Kinshasa, which was threatened by the advance of rebel forces under Laurent Kabila.

All pretence at law and order had broken down in the power vacuum left by Mobutu's flight. The streets were full of looting government troops – whose failure to receive their wages was one of the causes of the collapse of the regime, and who became more nervous by the day at reports of Kabila's rapid victories over their comrades in the east of the country. In anticipation of bloody fighting for the capital, troops from France, Belgium, Portugal, Britain and the USA were standing by in Brazzaville, the capital of the former French Congo, opposite Kinshasa on the north bank of the Congo river. In the event Kinshasa fell into Kabila's hands without bloodshed, and intervention was not necessary.

Instead, heavy fighting broke out in June 1997 in Brazzaville itself, between three different factions eager for power in this oil-rich territory. The leaders were President Pascal Lissouba, who had won an election against former president Denis Sassou-Nguesso in August 1992; Sassou-

Nguesso; and Bernard Kolelas, the mayor of Brazzaville. Lissouba had at his disposal the regular army, but as this was disproportionately recruited from former president Sassou-Nguesso's Mbochi tribe he distrusted its loyalty. To be on the safe side he created a personal 'Zulu' militia (in name only – the real Zulus' homeland obviously lies thousands of kilometers away in South Africa), who were trained and equipped with the help of Israeli instructors. Sassou-Nguesso had his own 'Cobra' militia; and Kolelas assembled a 'Ninja' militia.

From June 1997 onwards these armed gangs clashed repeatedly. On 6 June armoured vehicles of the Congolese army – most of which did in fact stay loyal to the legitimate president – tried unsuccessfully to capture Sassou-Nguesso's residence in pursuit of the government's attempt to disband the private militias. In response Sasso-Nguesso's Cobras attacked the centre of Brazzaville and the airport, which were held by regular troops and Zulu militiamen. Within hours it became clear that President Lissouba was not in a position to

(Below) At Brazzaville airport légionnaires of the 4e Cie., 2e REI escort refugees to a waiting Transall. Note that the soldiers, in body armour and Spectra helmets, are forming a living shield all round the civilians – a necessary precaution, since the militias were still exchanging fire across the airport. Among the weapons visible here is a LRAC 89mm launcher as well as FAMAS and FR F-2 rifles.

(**Right**) A Legion para of 1er Cie., 2e REP on guard at the French embassy. Note that he has a 40mm rifle grenade mounted on the muzzle of his FAMAS; these weapons, with a range of about 100m, proved their worth in the counter-attack following the ambush on men of 3e Cie. on 7 June 1997. Under French tactical doctrine the issue of these grenades – which include armour-piercing as well as fragmentation rounds – takes the place of a one-shot disposable light LAW at squad level. When they are used up the rifleman can continue to use his FAMAS with conventional ammunition.

(**Below**) This VBL from the 2e REI was in fact used by the company commander of the 1er Cie., 2e REP. It was photographed in front of the Hotel Cosmos in Brazzaville, where refugees gathered. As it lay in the centre of the city, however, it was a favourite target for the warring factions, and was hit many times.

(Left) Légionnaires of the 4e Cie., 2e REI watching BM-21 rockets being fired over their positions by Congolese troops on the other side of the airport. That they are wearing their helmets instead of the much preferred beret, and the heavy and uncomfortable anti-splinter armour vests, shows that they are taking this situation seriously.

(Opposite) This VAB squad from 2e REI organise the evacuation of a Catholic school, watching for trouble from any direction as the civilians are brought out to the vehicle carrying only their most valued possessions.

(Below) A VBL and a VAB at Brazzaville railway station; the crews are tense behind their .50cal machine guns. The highly visible French flag is flown as a deterrent to the militias whose crossfire these légionnaires are braving. They have reason to be watchful: only a matter of seconds after these vehicles left the square three mortar bombs landed in it.

control the fighting which he himself had unleashed. Militiamen concentrated around their leaders; there was extensive looting; and elements of the army and navy went over to Sasso-Nguesso on 7 June.

Within less than three days heavy fighting spread throughout Brazzaville. One feature was unusual for these endemic African civil wars: the large number of armoured vehicles involved. During the Cold War, Congo-Brazzaville had served the Russians as a supply base for their infiltration of Angola; they had stock-piled heavy equipment there, and had provided military aid to the local army. From the latter's barracks there now emerged T-55 tanks, BTR-60 armoured personnel carriers and ZSU-23-4 self-propelled AA cannon.

Some 2,200 French and 400 other Western civilians were trapped in this spreading chaos, with supplies running out and in serious danger from the wild firing of the drugged-up militias. The CEA of the 2e REP had remained in Brazzaville after the aborted Operation Pelican I. On 7 June a patrol on its way to evacuate French citizens from the city centre was fired upon by the Zulu militia; one légionnaire was killed and seven wounded. The paras counter-attacked and killed 15 militiamen; but the situation was obviously intolerable, and Paris launched Operation Pelican II.

A 400-strong advance party of légionnaires, marines and artillery was flown in to the airport; these were soon reinforced, and in the end General Landrin had some 1,300 men

at his disposal, divided between three tactical headquarters (EMTs). EMT 2e REP, under Colonel Puga, was based at the Botanical Gardens; EMT 8e RPIMa held the southern part of the airport; and nearby EMT 1er REC, under Colonel Clement Bollée, was stationed at the Aéroclub, which was also the HQ of the French force. Each EMT had two infantry combat companies and a platoon of ERC 90 Sagaies; three 120mm mortars of 2e/68e RAA stood ready to deliver fire missions, and air support was within range from Mirage F-1CTs stationed at Bangui in the Central African Republic. Apart from the 2e REP elements the Legion units involved were the 4e Cie., 2e REI and the 2e Esc., 1er REC.

The French troops were ordered to maintain strict neutrality between the warring factions; their task was to rescue Western civilians and to defend them if necessary, but not to take sides – and the légionnaires were naturally quite undiscriminating in their low opinion of the militias. The front lines of the Cobra militia were only 200m north-west of the Aéroclub headquarters; on the other side of the runway lay the air force base, in the hands of the regular army, whose BM-21 and ZSU-23-4 fired on the Cobras directly over the heads of the French. Neither side had any fire discipline, which made it extremely difficult for General Landrin to protect the on-going evacuation airlift. The runway was defended by two platoons of the 1er REC's armoured cars, and despite unabated fire the C-130 Hercules and C-160 85

(Left) This légionnaire of the 1er Cie., 2e REP has a laser sight fitted to his FAMAS – one of about a dozen provided to men of the company during Operation Pelican II. This device proves itself best in house-to-house fighting, where targets are often fleeting; the projection of the laser target point gives quicker acquisition, quicker firing, and higher likelihood of a first-shot hit – which is what the Legion are trained to achieve. The psychological effect, on Third World opponents who still have a lively belief in witchcraft, was also valuable: as soon as they saw the red dot of the laser touch them they believed that their situation was already hopeless. They themselves tended to fire wildly at anything that moved without using their sights.

(Below left) The pennant on this aerial marks the vehicle as that of 'Soleil' – 'Sun', the traditional callsign of the commanding officer, here Colonel Puga of EMT 2e REP at Brazzaville.

(Opposite top) MILAN installation of the 4e Cie., 2e REI on top of an improvised bunker at the airport. When the photo was taken the MILAN was targeted in readiness on three T-55 tanks of the Cobra militia at the northern end of the runway; but it was also ready to take on a ZSU-23-4 of the Zulu militia at the southern end. This ATGW system can locate armoured targets at 4,000m and engage them at 2,000m; its hollow charge warhead has no problem in piercing armour much thicker than that of an elderly T-55.

(Opposite bottom) A Sagaie of the 1er Esc., 1er REC secures the taxiway while a C-130 Hercules lifts off with another load of evacuated civilians. The six ERC 90 and five P4 cross-country vehicles of the 1er REC were flown in on board four C-130s, and secured the landing strip immediately they deplaned.

Transalls continued to land and take off. So, each night, did an Antonov 12 bringing in supplies for President Lissouba's forces, which drew the fire of the militias – as did the C-130s and C-160s which they often mistook for it.

The majority of the battles between the militias took place in the centre of the city, where the 2e REP were responsible for searching for Western civilians and escorting them to four assembly points: the French embassy (which lay directly on one of the main battle lines), the Orstom Botanical Gardens (HQ of EMT 2e REP), the residence of the French ambassador on the bank of the river Congo, and the Aéroclub headquarters at the airport. Those who wished to leave the country were taken to the airport and flown out to Libreville in Gabon.

During one of these missions the 1er Section of 3e/2e REP were ambushed, losing one man killed and three badly wounded; Captain Trotignon nevertheless ordered his men to hold their fire, and tried to parley with the rebels. However, when the ambulances arrived to rescue the wounded only a few moments later they too were brought under fire; and this act of barbarity was immediately punished. Well-aimed rifle grenades quickly put the Congolese to flight; among the several dead they left behind was a high-ranking officer. The 2e REP were not troubled again; and another exchange of fire by the 2e REI at the airport was the only other incident during this phase.

Operation Pelican II officially ended at 1800 hours on 15 June, when the last civilians were flown out and the French units began to withdraw to the airport. In 60 rotations of the transport aircraft some 5,900 civilians had been evacuated; a further 16 rotations were required for the extraction of the French troops. The paras of 2e REP came under 81mm mortar fire while withdrawing from the Botanical Gardens, but they reached the airport without further casualties.

(Above) Flown in for Pelican II without much transport, the French troops requisitioned many four-wheel-drives locally to improve their mobility. This one, originally the property of a French civilian who had already been flown out of Brazzaville, is being used by the CEA, 2e REP. All the doors, the windscreen and the roof have been removed to allow quicker entry and exit. Armour vests were often slung along the sides of such vehicles to give a measure of protection against small arms and splinters.

(Left) Men of the 4e Cie., 2e REI try to spot the source of the shots which have just hit their position.

(Right) At the airport members of the crew of a 1er REC Sagaie prepare 7.62mm link for their co-axial machine gun. As this photo was taken intensive fire was to be heard from all around. The locals were normally very bad shots, but their aim was so wild that the danger from 'shorts' was considerable when they fired at each other from either side of the airport.

(Below) A column of vehicles pass through the apparently deserted inner city of Brazzaville; a looted shop burns in the background, and stray bullets whistle around the vehicles. The rules of engagement prevented the légionnaires from returning fire unless they came under direct attack. For this reason all three local militias made a practice of firing at one another across any French troops as soon as they appeared, in the hope that their enemies would hit the French when they fired back and thus attract the Legion's firepower onto themselves.

5e Régiment Étranger

The 5e Régiment Étranger d'Infanterie was formed in September 1930 from three battalions of the 1er REI then in garrison in Tonkin (North Vietnam); the 5e RE still bears the nickname 'Régiment de Tonkin'. Under the Vichy regime the garrison of French Indochina were forced to accept Japanese occupation; but in March 1945 the Japanese suddenly turned on the French troops. Most of the 5e REI made an 800km (500-mile) fighting retreat through jungle mountains into China. After fighting communist guerrillas in Laos in 1946 the regiment was disbanded, but was reformed again in 1949. The 5e fought throughout the Indochina War, and was the last French regiment to leave Vietnam in 1956; on its return it was immediately committed to the Algerian War. After Algerian independence in 1962 the 5e was posted across the world to Tahiti in the French Polynesian islands.

In October 1963 the unit was transformed into the 5e Régiment Mixte du Pacifique, a mixed Legion/Engineer regiment; the present title was adopted in 1984. The 5e RMP set up and maintained all the regional test and support facilities of the Direction des Centres d' Expérimentation Nucleaire in Tahiti and on Muroroa, Hao and Rah atolls. They ran the vehicle depot, drinking water supplies, power plants, and loading and unloading of all material shipped and flown in; took responsibility for all engineering tasks througout the Polynesian region; and secured the nuclear sites against unauthorised entry.

In mid-1998 France agreed to cease its underground nuclear tests in the region, and DIRCEN has closed the Muroroa facility. Today the 5e RE comes under COMSUP, and is stationed on Hao atoll, some 900km (560 miles) from Tahiti and 19,000km (11,800 miles) from France. The unit was reduced to two companies: the Compagnie de Commandement, de Base et de Soutien (Command, Base & Supply Co.), and Compagnie de Travaux (Works Company). At the time of writing the latter was being replaced by a rotating company from either the 6e REG or the non-Legion 17th Parachute Engineer Regiment from France.

The Polynesian atolls are France's last base in the Pacific, and the unit's task is to maintain infrastructure for the reception of intervention forces in case of emergency. It retains its regional engineer mission; for instance, over seven months of 1996-97 the 5e built an airstrip on Ahe atoll.

(Opposite) Breast and beret badges of the 5e RE. The former incorporates the Legion's red and green and the seven-flame grenade; from the French army Engineers branch, the colour black (also a reference to the sacrifices suffered in Tonkin) and the traditional siege helmet; and flanking *tikis* referring to its station in Polynesia.

(Right) Since 9 December 1963 the 5e RMP and 5e RE have carried the flag of the 5e REI, disbanded in November that year. Like all Legion regimental colours this tricolour bears the motto 'Honneur et Fidelité' ('Honour and Loyalty'), and the regimental battle honours. The 5e REI was awarded the Croix de Guerre TOE in Indochina in 1950; the medal is pinned to the flag, and all ranks wear the pale blue and red lanyard at the left shoulder. (Photo *Képi Blanc*)

(Opposite) In spite of the fact that the légionnaires are often at sea for days at a time and may be stationed on far-flung atolls for long periods, neither training nor tradition are neglected. In remote corners of the earth and in extreme climatic conditions unit cohesion has an even greater value than at home. The regimental march of the 5e is *'Le front haut et l'âme fière'* ('Head up and soul proud'). Music and singing on the march are very important in the Legion; they contribute to the ésprit de corps of the different regiments, and even some individual companies have their own special songs. About one third of the songs sung by the Legion today are of German origin (with new French words), due to the large numbers of German volunteers following the end of World War II. (Photo *Képi Blanc*)

(Left) Amphibious operations are still carried out in conjunction with the French navy, and if called upon to intervene in an emergency the 5e could put a combat company into the field. Here légionnaires board a landing craft for a combat exercise on one of the French Polynesian atolls. (Photo *Képi Blanc*)

4e Régiment Étranger

The 4e Régiment Étranger d'Infanterie was formed in Morocco in 1920 from battalions of the 1er and 2e RE. It was heavily involved in the pacification campaigns of the 1920s and early 1930s, and remained in garrison thereafter, earning the nickname 'Régiment de Maroc'; one battalion also distinguished itself during the Druze revolt in Syria. Disbanded in 1940, it passed its flag and traditions to a new 4e Demi-Brigade which served in Senegal. Returning to North Africa in December 1942 after the Allied 'Torch' landings, the 4e DBLE joined a hastily organised 1er REI de Marche, fighting the Afrika Korps in Tunisia in May 1943. It was soon disbanded again, its men passing into the new RMLE which fought in Europe in 1944-45.

Reformed in Morocco in May 1946, the 4e DBLE became the 4e REI once more in October 1947. One battalion served in Madagascar from 1947 to 1951. Trouble broke out in Morocco in 1952; the regiment was continually involved in police actions until Moroccan independence was granted. In April 1957 it was the last Legion unit to leave Morocco;

thereafter it fought as a motorised intervention regiment until the end of the Algerian War in 1962, remaining in the Saharan concession bases until disbanded in 1964.

The flag and traditions of the 4e were taken over by the Régiment d'Instruction de la Légion Étrangere (RILE), set up in September 1977 to take over the central training function from the former GILE of the 2e REI. The title changed to 4e Régiment Étranger in June 1980. Today the 4e RE, based at the Quartier Capitaine Danjou at Castelnaudary, France, is responsible for all légionnaire and NCO training. The unit is organised into a Command & Services Co. (CCS); three

(Top of page) Breast and beret badges of the 4e RE. The former, worn since the 1930s by the 4e REI in Morocco, incorporates the *koutoubia* of Marrakech and in the background the slopes of the Atlas Mountains.

(Below) Drill teaches the recruits to obey orders exactly and immediately; singing the Legion's songs helps their instruction in the French language; both build self-esteem, team spirit, and a respect for tradition.

(**Left**) During basic training the cross-country marching performance of the would-be légionnaire is continuously increased. As well as group marches with full equipment and pack, individual recruits have to complete orienteering marches on their own. The training is deliberately severe; any man who volunteers for the Legion knows that he will be pushed to the limit by bellowing instructors, and it is only in this way that men from many different countries and backgrounds can be motivated to give everything they have got to the team.

Foreign Volunteer Cos. for basic training (1er, 2e, 3e CEV); a Cadre Training Co. for NCOs' instruction (CIC); and a Specialist Training Company (CIS).

The four-month basic training makes légionnaires out of the recruits selected by the 1er RE at Aubagne. Three strands stand out: the recruit learns the French language, his physical fitness is brought up to the required level, and, in accordance with the maxim 'Every légionnaire is an infantryman', he receives extensive training as a combat rifleman. The instructors, most of them NCOs with battle experience, form the trainees into mixed groups of French-speakers and others, so that the gradually-acquired knowledge of the French language

will be practised daily. At Castelnaudary the recruit learns the basics of military life: marching and drilling, rank recognition, military order and discipline, weapons handling, etc.

Part of his instruction takes place at one of three training grounds at Corbiéres and the Montagne Noire; here he will make punishing marches across country in full pack, and carry out combat exercises. During this phase all contact with the outside world is cut off and the recruits are reliant on themselves – even cooking is done at squad level – so that the individual's ability to operate as a member of a team can be assessed. An unsatisfactory recruit's contract can be cancelled at any time during these four weeks. At the end of basic train-

ing, in a torch-lit evening ceremony, the successful recruits are reminded of their duty as légionnaires; *'Le Boudin'* is sung; and they put on their white képis for the first time. From this moment the recruit is accepted into the Legion family.

The Compagnie d'Instruction des Cadres trains those selected in both general and specialist NCO duties. The main emphasis is upon leadership, abilities as an instructor, and accurate knowledge of and competence in essential combat techniques. The corporals' course lasts nine weeks, the sergeants' course 15 weeks. A légionnaire or corporal will only be sent on these courses by his unit if he shows definite leadership potential by his own physical fitness, enthusiasm for action, attention to duties, obedience to regulations and respect for the traditions of the Legion.

The Compagnie d'Instruction des Spécialistes gives 40 courses per year in administrative and technical skills. The courses last between three and 16 weeks, and about 600 légionnaires and NCOs pass through them annually.

(Left & below) Starting with this type of very basic obstacle course and progressing through ever greater challenges, the CEVs of the 4e RE increase the recruit's physical fitness to levels which he had never expected of himself. The experience of having been able to endure more than he had ever believed himself capable of, in extreme circumstances such as bad weather or injuries, may one day mean the difference between life or death for the légionnaire.

(Right) In the Compagnie d'Instruction des Spécialistes a wide range of technical courses are available; here an NCO instructs two trainees in engine maintenance. All vehicle mechanics are trained at the 4e RE before transferring to their units all over the world. They must be competent to maintain in working order a fleet including everything from the old jeep to the most modern VAB and AMX armoured fighting vehicles – often in extreme conditions of weather and terrain, and far from rear echelon facilities.

(Below) The trainee will make many cross-country runs in full equipment before qualifying for his white képi. Over the four-month period the distances will be increased from 7km (4.35 miles) to 21km (13 miles). The climax is a 25km (15.5 miles) run with a 15kg (33lb) rucksack.

(Left) Basic training has to form individuals of many different cultures into the larger Legion family; order, discipline, punctuality and cleanliness are required, and NCOs do not tolerate carelessness in these matters. Here an instructor inspects an eight-man barrack room. The locker, in which the man's entire equipment is stowed away, must be ready for a snap inspection at any moment. A single shelf is available for all a recruit's personal possessions.

(Right) Instruction in operating with helicopters - here the standard Puma troop transport variant – forms a part of both the second half of a légionnaire's basic training, and the NCO courses run by the CIC at Castelnaudary. These phases are co-ordinated, so that the NCO candidates can be tested on their own training capability in the new techniques. The CEVs teach the basics of movement by helicopter; the CIC teaches NCOs to supervise the preparation of their squads for helicopter transport – the load capacities of the various types, the preparation of equipment, ground/air communications, etc. – together with the direction of the aircraft and reconnoitering of landing zones.

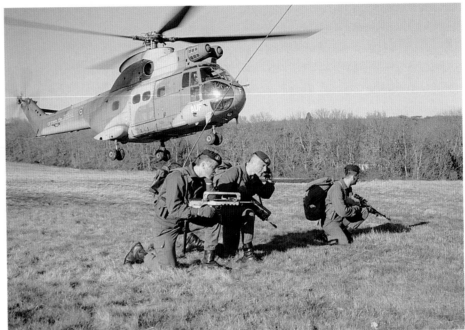

(Left) Weapons handling is obviously one of the essential components of basic training. Recruits are instructed in all the standard infantry weapons; whatever their eventual posting, they must all be competent combat riflemen before arriving at their unit. They are trained on the FAMAS assault rifle, FN FR-2 sniper's rifle, Minimi light machine gun, LRAC anti-armour weapon and hand grenades.